Call of the Infinite

The Way of Shin Buddhism

'This book takes on the big questions of human existence—Who am I? What am I here for? Where am I going? How can I live my life to the full, with the wisdom of knowing the way things are and with compassion for all beings? It then leads the reader to discover answers from the perspective of the Shin Buddhist path. This is a timely work for troubled times, with a refreshing message and vision for our twenty-first century global society.'

[Prof. Ruben L.F. Habito, Founding Teacher, Maria Kannon Zen Center, Dallas, author of *Experiencing Buddhism: Ways of Wisdom and Compassion.*]

'Following the traditional Buddhist pattern of diagnosis and treatment, *Call of the Infinite* probes the perplexities of the modern human condition and offers the teachings of Shin Buddhism as a plausible, indeed powerful, response. Common presentations of Buddhist practice as an impersonal process of stripping away our human nature are exposed as limited, and the author quarries the rich spiritual, emotional and aesthetic resources of the Pure Land tradition—from deep within the heart of the Mahayana—enabling them to speak clearly and effectively to the contemporary spiritual seeker. A truly beautiful book.'

[Dr Wendy Dossett, Director, Religious Experience Research Centre, University of Wales at Lampeter.]

'This accessible, elegant and penetrating interpretation of the essential teachings of Shin Buddhism is a significant addition to the slender body of Western writings on a little-understood branch of the Buddhist tradition. Lucid and sometimes provocative, this book is an invitation to the profound spiritual experience which can be found through time-tested methods available to any sincere wayfarer.'

[Prof. Harry Oldmeadow, La Trobe University, Bendigo, author of *Journeys East: 20th Century Western Encounters with Eastern Religious Traditions.*]

'This presentation of the Shin Buddhist teachings addresses universal spiritual concerns in a way that leaves readers reassured and wanting to know more. Paraskevopoulos' writing is luminous and soothing, as if one were reading poetry. As a pioneer of Shin Buddhism in Australia, he offers fresh insights rarely seen in Japan. His treatment, in particular, of the importance of beauty to our spiritual life is inspirational.'

[Prof. Kenneth K. Tanaka, Musashino University, Tokyo, President, International Association of Shin Buddhist Studies, author of *Ocean: An Introduction to Jodo Shinshu Buddhism in America.*]

'Paraskevopoulos has pondered Shinran's thought with forthrightness and has written an eloquent meditation on questions that arise in a contemporary engagement with the Pure Land path. Drawing on a generous range of traditional sources, he explores the practical implications of the Shin Buddhist challenge to modern conceptions of the self.'

[Prof. Dennis Hirota, Ryukoku University, Kyoto, co-author of *Shinran: An Introduction to His Thought.*]

'This splendid book is uplifting, inspiring, accurate, authentic and positive. The work of a knowledgeable authority, *Call of the Infinite* exemplifies the affirmative dimension of Buddhism—that which reveals the Buddha's ever-present and ever-beneficent Great Self—in contrast to the joyless negativism that commonly usurps the Buddhist name. Thoroughly and unreservedly recommended.'

[Dr Tony Page, Bangkok University, editor of the *Mahayana Mahaparinirvana Sutra.*]

CALL OF THE INFINITE

The Way of Shin Buddhism

John Paraskevopoulos

SOPHIA PERENNIS

First published in the USA
by Sophia Perennis

Revised Edition by Sophia Perennis,
an imprint of Angelico Press 2017

Series editor: James R. Wetmore

For information, address:
4709 Briar Knoll Dr.
Kettering, OH 45429
www.@angelicopress.com
info@angelicopress.com

Library of Congress Cataloging-in-Publication Data

Paraskevopoulos, John.
The way of Shin Buddhism / John Paraskevopoulos.

p. cm.
Includes bibliographical references.
ISBN 978-1-62138-245-4 (pbk: alk. paper)
ISBN 978-1-62138-246-1 (cloth: alk. paper)
ISBN 978-1-59731-174-8 (ebook)
1. Shin (Sect)—Doctrines. 2. Pure Land Buddhism—Doctrines.
I. Title
BQ8718.5.P37 2009
294.3'926—dc22 2009047653

Cover design by Tony McKenzie, Yellow Moon Multimedia
Photograph ('Morning Clouds') courtesy of Photos8.com
Calligraphy (*Namo Amida Butsu*) by Rev. Zuiken S. Inagaki (1885–1981).

CONTENTS

This book is dedicated to my mother, Nicoleta, for her unstinting courage in the face of seeming hopelessness and for the untold kindnesses bestowed on so many, when life has afforded her so few.

For those who are ready,
The door to the deathless state is open.
You that have ears,
Give up the conditions that bind you
And enter in.

—*Majjhima Nikaya*

PREFACE

The following work introduces readers to some of the principal themes of Shin Buddhism, which belongs to the broader Pure Land tradition of the Mahayana. It is the largest school of Buddhism in Japan today, where it is known as *Jodo Shin.* Its founder was Shinran (1173–1263), a bold and innovative thinker who gave hope to ordinary people by making the teachings of the Buddha immediately relevant to their lives.

This book addresses the general reader who has an interest in spiritual matters as well as a philosophical outlook on life. However, we have avoided technical terms as much as possible and have used language that is simple and accessible. A background in Buddhism is not presupposed and suggestions for further reading are provided at the end for those wishing to explore these teachings in greater depth. In this respect, the book is not a work of scholarship but rather a contemplative and devotional study of what lies at the heart of this important Buddhist tradition. It seeks to provide an interpretation rather than mere analysis.

While aiming to impart a sense of how Shin can be meaningful to people living in the world today, we are also keen to present a vision of Buddhism with which some readers may be unfamiliar. Not the severe and forbidding religion that many suppose but, rather, a joyful journey filled with light—a challenging but enriching adventure of the spirit.

J.P.
Kyoto
Bodhi Day 2008

ACKNOWLEDGEMENTS

The author would like to express his appreciation for the assistance rendered by the following people. A deep debt of gratitude is owed to the Reverend George Gatenby for his sage counsel and constant encouragement during the preparation of this work. Many thanks are also due to Ms. Rosemary Moore and Professor Harry Oldmeadow for their valuable insights and editorial suggestions which helped to improve this work considerably, as well as to the Reverend Dr. Mark Healsmith and Mr. Graham Ranft for their very useful comments. I would also like to express my indebtedness to the International Association of Buddhist Culture in Kyoto for its generous publication grant.

The opportunity to write this work in Japan was made possible by the award of a Numata Fellowship between September and December 2008. The author would like to thank the Numata Foundation for its munificent support and Professor Mitsuya Dake of Ryukoku University for his kind assistance during the fellowship period.

CHAPTER ONE

Pain and Longing

The blossom that opens in the morning is scattered by the evening breeze, and the dew, condensed in hours of darkness before dawn, is dispelled by the rays of the morning sun. Heedless or willfully ignorant of this procession of changes, we dream of prosperity all through life and, without understanding the nature of transience, hope for longevity. All the while, across the face of the earth moves the restless wind of impermanence, dissolving all that it touches.

—*Honen*

Pain and Longing

If we ponder the matter seriously, it is difficult to avoid the conclusion that our life in this world is a profound mystery. Indeed, depending on the kind of person one is and the life one has led, it can also be wonderful, gratifying, anxious, miserable or simply an object of indifference. Regardless of our attitude to life, there remains something fundamentally inexplicable about our individual situation in the world. We have no say in who our parents are or the conditions into which we are born. Neither can we do much about our natural endowments. The variety of human temperaments and aptitudes is endless, as is the plethora of circumstances that influence our uncertain destinies.

Eventually, a reflective person will be prompted to ask searching questions about their life with a view to understanding its meaning. Why are we here? Do our lives have any purpose? Does it matter if they do not? What should our priorities be in the very short time we have on this planet? Of course, many people find some measure of fulfilment in raising a family, following a particular career or creative vocation, falling in love, helping others and so forth. These are noble and meaningful endeavours that can enrich our lives.

Yet, despite our varied attempts at seeking fulfilment, we often find ourselves disappointed. Either we are confronted by insurmountable obstacles in pursuing our goals or we find that the level of satisfaction for which we were hoping is never realised. In other words, our initial expectations are seldom met, so we feel let down. When life fails to meet our hopes and desires, we suffer. We suffer when things do not go our way or change suddenly, such as we find with relationships, health or financial security. We also suffer when we have to endure violence, cruelty, greed, prejudice, dishonesty or ignorance in the world.

We are not deliberately setting out to commence this book on a pessimistic note but acknowledging, at the outset, a fundamental, self-evident and inescapable fact about the human condition. This realisation came to the historical Buddha (also known as *Shakyamuni*—'Sage of the Shakya clan') 2500 years ago, who thought this insight so important that he made it the bedrock of his teaching. Why did he do this? Why focus on the negative aspects of life? Because he understood that coming to terms with suffering, disappointment and anguish was critical to uncovering its underlying meaning. By helping us see the implications of viewing life as unsatisfactory (a state of *dis-ease*), Shakyamuni could then clear the way to introduce his more positive teaching about wisdom, compassion, enlightenment and Nirvana.

Despite the all-pervasive nature of impermanence in our world, the human ego finds it very difficult to accept. Nothing could be more natural, it seems, than the state of constant flux in which we find all things. They are, as the *Diamond Sutra* states, 'like dreams, illusions, bubbles, shadows; like dew drops or a flash of lightning'. Yet we invariably tend to resist this truth by trying to make the objects of our desire last in ways that are not possible; this is yet another cause of suffering.

It is also natural for us to form attachments to people, animals, possessions and ways of life. We want to hold on to those things that we love and value, and to keep at bay the forces that seek to deprive us of them. However, death, illness and calamity are never far away and, even if we have been spared their ravages for the time being, the very fear that we may be next is a source of acute anxiety in itself.

This leads us to another fact about our human condition: it is frail and brittle. Hence, we find ourselves looking for ways to feel secure and shield our vulnerabilities. We are also beset by apprehension as the spectre of old age, death and oblivion hangs over us, even if this is not always consciously acknowledged. We desire what we do not have, and yet dread losing those very things once we get them, only to find that they too fall short of giving us the fulfilment for which we so desperately long.

One of the fundamental scriptures of Shin Buddhism is the *Sutra on the Buddha of Infinite Life.*[1] In it, we find a very vivid account of the parlous state of humanity:

> People of the world, being weak in virtue, engage in strife over matters that are not urgent. In the midst of abject wickedness and extreme afflictions, they painstakingly toil for their living. Whether noble or corrupt, rich or poor, young or old, male or female, all people worry about wealth and property. In this, there is no difference between the rich and the poor; both have their anxieties. Groaning in dejection and sorrow, they pile up thoughts of anguish or, driven by inner urges, they run wildly in all directions and thus have no time for peace and rest. . . .
>
> Gnawing grief afflicts them and incessantly troubles their hearts. Anger seizes their minds, keeps them in constant agitation, increasingly tightens its grip, hardens their hearts and never leaves them . . . they drink bitterness and eat hardship. . . .

1. The origins of the Pure Land sutras are shrouded in mystery but it is traditionally accepted that they were rooted in the enlightenment of the historical Buddha even if they were not delivered in the exact form in which we have received them today. Indeed, it is quite credible to suppose that the fundamental insights of the Pure Land teaching were maintained and transmitted orally over many generations after the time of Shakyamuni, prior to their written codification much later in the course of history. During the period of this transmission, the tradition itself developed and refined the teaching further in light of the spiritual experience of its sages.

> When their lives end in such agonising conditions, they must leave everybody and everything behind. Even nobles and men of wealth have these worries. With much anxiety and fear, they endure such tribulation. . . .
>
> In the midst of worldly desires and attachments, one comes and goes alone, is born alone and dies alone. . . .
>
> The reality of birth-and-death is such that the sorrow of parting is mutually felt by all generations. Parents mourn the death of their children; children mourn the death of their parents. Brothers, sisters, husbands and wives mourn each other's deaths. According to the basic law of impermanence, whether death will occur in order of seniority or in the reverse is unpredictable. All things must pass. Nothing stays forever. Few believe this, even if someone teaches and exhorts them. . . .
>
> Because they are deeply troubled and confused, people indulge their passions. Everyone is restlessly busy, having nothing on which to rely. Whether moral or corrupt, of high or low rank, rich or poor, noble or base, all are preoccupied with their own work. They entertain venomous thoughts, creating a widespread and dismal atmosphere of malevolence. . . .
>
> People are deluded by their passionate attachments, unaware of the Way, misguided and trapped by anger and enmity, and intent on gaining wealth and gratifying their carnal desires like wolves. How miserable and pitiable this is!

Suffering is also inherent in our experience of pleasure. Shakyamuni observed that, despite our relentless pursuit of all things pleasant and desirable, the reality of impermanence ensures that they do not always remain so and, with their passing, we suffer for the loss of those pleasures that made us happy. We also know the feeling of dissatisfaction even when we succeed in obtaining what we thought we wanted. It was for good reason that Shakyamuni insisted that there were no lasting pleasures in this 'burning house', as he characterised our world of endless craving and frustration.

Shakyamuni helps us to understand what it means to suffer and to realise how precarious and unsettled our lives really are. So, in the face of all this disappointment in the struggle for contentment, what can impermanence teach us? What does it mean to be fulfilled and happy?

Let us examine more closely our very human response to suffering and the realities of our troubled existence. We have already touched on such feelings as fear, despair and vulnerability. These reactions are familiar to all of us even if we do not care to recognise them in ourselves. If we look a little deeper, we may also find that, at the core of our being, there lies an intense longing for that which is stable, certain, reliable and free from suffering.

To be sure, the world does not furnish us with any immediate examples of what might meet these criteria but the fact remains that we long for such qualities anyway. For no sooner do we think we have found happiness, than it is swiftly taken from us – sometimes gradually and imperceptibly, sometimes violently. And yet our desire for that which is not fleeting and perishable remains unabated. We persist—despite the seemingly overwhelming evidence to the contrary—in this irresistible yearning for something immutable.

This creates a strange and disconcerting predicament, peculiar to the experience of human beings. Why do we yearn for that which our experience of the world suggests does not exist? Are we even looking in the right place?

The innate desire (indeed insistence) of children to see fairy tales conclude with a happy ending is very telling. Why this expectation given what many children already know to be the case about the realities of life? People are often embarrassed to acknowledge this kind of longing as they believe it will expose them to the ridicule of their peers, revealing them as somehow naïve or unsophisticated, but it is important to overcome these inhibitions and follow the leads wherever they take us.

Consider the case of love and desire in general. Our capacity for both appears to be boundless. Despite the countless setbacks and disappointments we encounter in our personal aspirations or ambitions, our fundamental ability to love and desire remains, for the most part, unimpaired. Is there anything significant in this? Does it point to a deeper aspect of our nature that requires an altogether different response? Or are we doomed to having our innate need for love remain unfulfilled? Can the evidently insatiable nature of desire ever be quelled?

Like our experience of hunger and thirst, this visceral yearning in the depths of our being intimates the existence of something that satisfies it and which meets the need that these powerful emotions elicit. Of course, unlike hunger and thirst, this basic demand of the human heart is not a physical necessity and therefore its object may seem elusive and uncertain. However, just like the essential requirements of our body, this longing that we feel constantly (even though it remains vague to us) indicates a real need that can be satisfied only by that which is enduring and steadfast; which is worthy of the depth and compelling nature of this intrinsic desire.

Unless we are prepared to believe that this vital need that we have is some kind of delusion, we must consider seriously whether our unflagging pursuit of ephemeral pleasures could be misguided. It may, in fact, point to a more fundamental kind of desire—spiritual in nature—that can only be met in other ways.

Of course, seeking out ordinary joys and pleasures in the world is a perfectly natural thing to do and, very often, rewarding. However, with their passing, we are sometimes left with a vague and uneasy sense of despondency; as if an initial promise has not been fulfilled or as though something remains unresolved that we continue to overlook. This feeling gently and subtly gnaws away at us as a reminder that we are neglecting something important—indeed critical—to our well-being. What could this be? How could something so obscure be that significant?

Our many and varied attachments to the things of this world make it very difficult to notice anything else apart from what we can see, touch, hear, taste and smell. For many of us, this is all that is real and talk of anything else is absurd. This is understandable, up to a point, but it fails to recognise the intangible dimensions of our being. The very vividness and intensity of our physical life can often blind us to an awareness of other experiences that may hold the key to understanding this deep yearning that we have.

It may be tempting to dismiss any talk of 'yearning' and 'longing' as the fabrication of an overly emotional or hyper-sensitive temperament. However, the fact remains that we cannot—if we are completely honest with ourselves—easily erase the sense of emptiness that follows our desperate grasping at false substitutes for that which is truly able to satisfy us. These might include, for example, more wealth, a prestigious career, a new lover, a beautiful house or greater social standing. Such objectives are not being dismissed as wrong; we just need to clearly recognise their limited ability to provide enduring satisfaction.

We spoke earlier of the widespread extent of suffering in the world; watching half an hour of news every evening should suffice to bring this point home without too much argument. Even if our lives seem mostly pain-free, we can nevertheless acknowledge that the lives of many others are riddled with misery and horror, and that such a fate could befall us in the blink of an eye.

We live under conditions that are marked by uncertainty and constant transition, where not just our environment but our very bodies and minds are always changing, with largely unpredictable consequences to our health, hopes and plans. This is a source of great trepidation in our lives; nothing really seems as solid, secure or dependable as we would like it to be.

Even those for whom we have the greatest love and deepest affection, or who have shown themselves to be the closest and most faithful of friends, will one day die. We can do nothing to keep them or to delay the bitter sadness of that final parting. Perhaps this is stating the obvious but we are often forgetful of these basic truths until they—suddenly, unexpectedly, shockingly—slap us hard in the face, as if to awaken us from a dream.

Many believe that pain and suffering are without any particular significance: simply unwanted realities that we must do our best to avoid. Of course, we are duty-bound to reduce the amount of distress and hardship in the world, although this is not always possible despite our best efforts. That said, however, the view is commonly held that there is no deeper meaning to life's grievous trials; that they are just a brute fact of existence that we have to accept along with the pleasant and joyous encounters in our lives.

Perhaps there is another way of viewing the matter. Although it may sound strange at first, we need to consider the possibility that adversity, misfortune and tragedy can be very important teachers. What they teach us is that the everyday world with its limitations, transitory pleasures and false hopes is, ultimately, unsatisfactory and should not be the object of our deepest aspiration. In other words, we should aim, instead, to place our confidence in that which lies beyond the hazardous and insecure realm of our evanescent world. This is not some escapist plea to flee from our duties and responsibilities in life; it simply means that we should not turn to the world—this 'burning house'—for our ultimate refuge.

It is as if our keen awareness of suffering and unhappiness is forcing us to look elsewhere for its resolution. Our fathomless desire for stability, permanence and certainty is, therefore, not some kind of wistful chimera. It suggests something very real and essential that the world is unable to provide. This impalpable sense of longing that we feel is a strong and forceful signal from our deeper self that this is a need that can, and must, be met if we are to live our lives to their fullest potential. Therefore, the consummation of this desire must lie in a dimension altogether different from the everyday conditions of ordinary life. So how are we to understand this mysterious reality that is being suggested as the goal of our quest? What, exactly, are we talking about?

When it dawns on us that the finite things of this world are incommensurate with our deepest yearning, we are prompted to consider the notion that what we are actually looking for, in fact, is that which is not limited, which is without pain, deficiency or imperfection: a reality unsullied by the flaws of mundane existence. In other words, what we are seeking is the *Infinite*—something that is recognisable in the finite, at the heart of all things, but which surpasses them. If we are able to look deeply into ourselves with clarity, we may come to see that we are inextricably linked to the Infinite, and that only through contact with it are we able to attain the kind of profound fulfilment that so distressingly eludes us in our lives.

Given the difficulty in understanding something so seemingly strange and remote, it is easy to be sceptical and to dismiss these intuitions as a trick of the mind. However, there are times when we need to question our scepticism. Awareness of something mysterious and numinous at the heart of life is a paramount experience of those who follow the great spiritual traditions of the world and, unless we are prepared to believe that the hundreds of millions of people throughout history who have believed in a higher reality were either liars or hopelessly misguided, then we need to take such claims seriously and give thought to their implications. Buddhism, too, subscribes to such a reality but approaches it in its own unique way, as we shall discover later.

Of course, the existence of an infinite and eternal reality has long been disputed by many thinkers who claim that there is no evidence for it. Indeed, it cannot be demonstrated to exist in the same way that objects in the world are shown to be real. It is, in a sense, too close to us and requires that we adopt a different manner of seeing in order to apprehend its presence. That said, the most convincing form of proof is to have a direct and immediate experience of this reality for oneself.

The testimony of those who have encountered the Infinite reveals that the power of their experience is such that it constitutes its own evidence; it comes with a sense of utter conviction which is impossible to doubt. A parent who answers 'Yes, absolutely' to the question, 'Do you love your child?' is scarcely able to add anything to that response if challenged to prove that it is true. Sometimes in life, the strength of certain insights or feelings is so great that they admit of no uncertainty. Indeed, the veracity of what is felt is often more compelling than that of many so-called 'factual' matters regarding the world.

Nevertheless, we must retain a firm command over our critical faculties and remain vigilant regarding experiences that, upon further reflection, might prove false or misleading. We should always keep an open mind and never fail to exercise the highest standards of intellectual rigour and probity where applicable. We must also ensure that our beliefs and actions do not oppress or cause harm to others. There is no shortage of examples—in the religious world especially—of fundamentalist thinking that is based, not so much on any intuitive awareness of the spiritually profound, but on a need to buttress an extreme ideology or to lend credence to an array of highly pernicious prejudices.

Of course, each person must decide the matter for themselves but, in doing so, it is crucial that we are not swayed by shallow considerations that blind us to the overwhelming testimony of humanity's great spiritual traditions and to our own deepest instincts.

Suffering is inevitable in a world that is imperfect and impermanent. We must accept this fact and not pretend that we can eliminate the miseries of life through utopian societies or endless social activism in the hope of bringing our worldly ills to an end. We should, by all means, endeavour to eliminate pain and injustice wherever we can, but it is not always clear how we are to do so. We must also concede that honourable intentions have sometimes compounded the very evils they were seeking to dispel.

Inaction or indifference in the face of adversity is not an option. However, let us apply any moral, social or political solutions to our problems with great humility, admitting their limitations and inability to address the fundamental problem of human suffering at its root. After all, it is not just the texture of the world that is flawed. We, too, form an integral part of this world and are likewise beset by a host of infirmities that so often prevent us from creating ideal communities of peace, harmony and compassion.

As much as some would want to resist it, the real solution to the problem of suffering may lie in a realm which, while embracing this world and essentially one with it, is nevertheless greater in every way. After all, what is it that enables us, in the first place, to recognise the shortcomings and deficiencies in our existence and to want to overcome them, if not the presence within each person of something that is limitless, unimpeded and conducive to the highest happiness? How else can we form a judgement about the nature of suffering and its undesirability if we have no conception of its opposite, which is so deeply woven into the fabric of our being? This fact should make us pause and reflect on the source of our most important convictions about life.

Given, therefore, the nature of the world in which we live, suffering is inescapable and cannot be conquered through any easy panaceas. We can certainly make a modest difference here and there, but the fact remains that suffering is endemic to our lives. However, in moments of reflection, we may come to see that we do not entirely belong to this ephemeral world of dissatisfaction. We are tightly bonded to a higher reality which, though intangible to our ordinary senses, discloses its presence in untold ways when we begin to awaken to it.

Although we can do little to prevail against the countless vicissitudes of life, we are able, by being firmly grounded on that which transcends this fugitive world, to put our sufferings in perspective. We continue to endure the ills of existence, along with everybody else, but we do not become completely overwhelmed or consumed by them as long as we remain open to the Eternal; in this lies our true liberation from the shackles of our earthly condition.

Are we saying, then, that true happiness is not possible? When asked what happiness means, people give a wide range of responses, as we have seen. Over time, many also end up revising their views on happiness, especially when experience has given them cause to reconsider the real basis of their welfare. We may eventually come to the view that happiness is not a very stable commodity; that it waxes and wanes according to our circumstances or state of mind. When we feel this way, we are prone to chase after something new—something, we hope, that is not as fickle as other things that have let us down in the past. Such hopes, alas, are often in vain.

To be sure, some pursuits are seen as inherently more exemplary or laudable than others. Few, perhaps, would put the life of the wanton hedonist on the same level as that of a self-effacing, under-paid nurse who works long hours looking after patients in a cancer ward. Yet doing something considered more worthy by others does not necessarily make one happier. Perhaps the very word 'happiness' is replete with ambiguity and needs to be refined a little. People can lead lives that are fulfilling even if they suffer many misfortunes. Others do not feel that their lives are terribly meaningful, despite finding pockets of joy or pleasure here and there that help to brighten an otherwise drab existence.

Of course, everyone wants to be happy but we are often so unsure about how and where to look for it. These days, we find ourselves repeatedly being told by others (invariably, companies and their advertising executives) what it will take for us to be fully content but, not surprisingly, such promises prove to be spurious as we come to realise the deceptive nature of the consumerist 'mantra'.

In the end, it remains true that we are not very clear about happiness, to the point where we think it is simply impossible to have. This may be because we are trying to seize it as a possession or a permanent acquisition. A doting mother may lose her child in some tragedy—suddenly, a life of rejoicing is reduced to unspeakable agony. A brilliant pianist whose sole joy is in thrilling audiences with her playing may permanently damage her hands in an accident. It is important to see that the things we love and to which we are profoundly attached, all those ventures that give our life a sense of purpose, can be taken from us abruptly and, with them, our feelings of happiness.

If we think more carefully about the examples just given, we find that even the most envied of lives is fraught with its own problems. What appears to be another's privileged or fortunate existence can be riddled with its own discontent (albeit well concealed from the gaze of others). Perhaps the mother who derives so much joy from her child has an abusive husband; the gifted musician may lead a life of desperate loneliness; our noble nurse may suffer from depression; a charismatic politician may be devoured by a tormenting ambition that can never be quenched; a famous celebrity may be plagued by a sense of inadequacy or self-loathing.

The examples we could cite are endless but the point is that no life is simply happy or unhappy. Our lives are often entwined with both elation and dismay, which makes any kind of final verdict on happiness very difficult. However, if we identify our well-being with a life that is meaningful and which connects us to something greater than ourselves, something that is impervious to the incessantly changing onslaught of circumstances and emotions to which we are all held captive, then we may be closer to finding what we are looking for.

It is this connection with a greater reality that is capable of lending our lives significance and direction even if our personal circumstances are not always happy. A life of meaning, as opposed to just pleasure or consumption, may come nearest to embodying the kind of existence that can help us surmount the limitations, failures and disappointments in our everyday lives – not by denying or rejecting them, but by putting them firmly in perspective through a higher awareness.

People seem hard-wired in such a way that the things of this world—the various desires and pursuits that we seek—singularly fail, in the end, to fully satisfy us. Even if we manage to acquire what we covet most in life, we still sense that something is missing. This is especially the case with those who have already secured some of those goods (e.g. wealth and fame) for which the rest of us may still be striving.

Once we have 'ticked all the boxes' in life, we will—sooner or later – be struck by the question: 'What does it all mean?' Is our objective merely to subsist, make money, consume and be comfortable as we await the inexorable onset of death? Is that it? Are we here for no other reason than to merely endure our lives—riding them out to the end, while restlessly chasing after this and that? To what purpose?

Surely, one could retort, we exist to experience wonderful things like love, kindness and human warmth. Wonderful they are, indeed, but not always dependable. Popular culture is rife with examples of the unhappiness caused by love lost or betrayed. Of course, we do not give up just because love has let us down but, again, we find that subsequent relationships are no less burdened with other problems or challenges.

The contentment we believe can be found—if only we keep searching hard enough—sometimes continues to elude us. Nevertheless, we also need to acknowledge that, despite these difficulties, people find great solace in human relationships and that the love, tenderness and trust that we are able to experience through them can often lead us to explore deeper spiritual dimensions in our lives.

We cannot doubt the need for commitment and devotion to our families, friends and community. Indeed, life would be even more of a struggle without such affection and loyalty. Even so, perhaps the existence of such elusive phenomena as love and beauty—which are so desired yet so transient in this life—suggests the presence of a realm from which they, along with even truth and wisdom, have their real origin.

At the time of his enlightenment, Shakyamuni became awakened to Nirvana—a state of unutterable happiness; an absence of sorrow. It was this, he declared, that is the final goal of all human endeavour, without which our lives would be incomplete. If we do not seek this highest of goods, he said, we are living beneath ourselves, destined for an unsatisfying existence.

> A life of addiction to desires or a life of pomp and vainglory cannot last long. All must pass. . . . It is time for all to seek deliverance from the pains of birth, death, old age and sickness. Outflows of depravity and defilement are everywhere, and there is nothing in which you can find true joy.
>
> —*Sutra on the Buddha of Infinite Life*

Strong sentiments, you might think, and ones likely to provoke a trenchant reaction from those who feel that their lives are perfectly fine, even if not perfect, without having to reach for such an inaccessible and seemingly implausible experience.

On one level, of course, it is natural to feel that what we encounter in our day-to-day lives is all there is—after all, these are tangible, vivid and immediate in a way that lofty spiritual states, of which one hears, may not be. Yet for those (not just the historical Buddha) for whom such phenomena are palpably real, there is no greater certainty. This infinite reality is experienced as truth, joy and bliss—our true home from which we have strayed and to which we can return.

In the next chapter, we will examine the nature of this reality—how we are to understand it and how we can approach it. If what is claimed about it is true, then it is vitally important to the quality of our lives that we awaken to it.

In Shin Buddhism, Nirvana or Ultimate Reality (also known as the 'Dharma-Body' or *Dharmakaya* in the original Sanskrit) has assumed a more concrete form as: (a) the Buddha of Infinite Light (*Amitabha*) and Eternal Life (*Amitayus*) and; (b) the 'Pure Land' or 'Land of Utmost Bliss' (*Sukhavati*), the realm over which this Buddha is said to preside. When Buddhism reached the Far East, this Buddha came to be known simply as *Amida* (the Japanese form of the Sanskrit word *amita*, meaning 'infinite' or 'immeasurable'). While Shin Buddhism makes a distinction between Amida Buddha and the Pure Land, they are—in effect—aspects of the same reality: the one formless and inconceivable world of Nirvana.

Amida is the Eternal Buddha who is said to have taken form as Shakyamuni and his teachings in order to become known to us in ways we can readily comprehend. As we shall see, many of the descriptions of Amida Buddha and the Pure Land in the sutras may strike the reader as rather fanciful and excessive, but it is important that we do not take these accounts too literally. They are powerful symbols intended to appeal to our spiritual imagination; to convey—in very rich and evocative imagery drawn from the everyday world of our senses—something of the Infinite to our limited understanding.

Let us now explore the world of Shin Buddhism, its conception of the highest reality, and what this means for us in the midst of our turbulent and afflicted lives.

CHAPTER TWO

Infinite Light

Suppose there is a room that has been dark for a thousand years. If light reaches it, however briefly, the room immediately becomes bright. How can the darkness say that, having occupied the room for a thousand years, it refuses to leave?

—*T'an-luan*

Infinite Light

The reality to which Shakyamuni awakened under the Bodhi Tree was described by him as *Nirvana.* While its literal meaning denotes 'blowing out' as in a flame (i.e. the fires of passion and delusion), its more positive connotation is that of a higher state of being, the dispelling of illusion and the corresponding joy of spiritual liberation. An early Buddhist scripture depicts Nirvana as:

> . . . . the far shore, the subtle, the very difficult to see, the unageing, the stable, the undisintegrating, the unmanifest, the peaceful, the deathless, the sublime, the auspicious, the secure, the destruction of craving, the wonderful, the amazing, the unailing, the unafflicted, dispassion, purity, freedom, the island, the shelter, the asylum, the refuge. . . .
>
> —*Samyutta Nikaya*

It is clear, when reading accounts of Shakyamuni's enlightenment, that this was not something he created through dint of mere personal effort. Certainly, he struggled and faced many trials and temptations in his spiritual quest but his final awakening was to something that lay beyond him; it was a higher realm into which he had penetrated or, rather, which had descended on him when he was ready to receive it. He did not bring into existence something that was not already there. Having realised enlightenment for himself, he became convinced that this truth was the key to human happiness and fulfilment, and thus resolved to share his experience with people from all walks of life, which he did for the next 45 years.

After some initial reluctance, Shakyamuni began to teach what he had discovered—the *Dharma.* At first, he despaired that the transcendent and inexpressible reality that was unveiled to him could be communicated in words but he persisted, encouraged by the prospect that some advanced souls might be able to fathom his teaching. However, Shakyamuni did not restrict his teaching to monks, nuns and scholars. He was also deeply concerned about the plight of ordinary people and sought to find ways to make the marvellous world of enlightenment available even to common folk who were preoccupied with their everyday lives, full of onerous cares, responsibilities and distractions. The Pure Land tradition of Buddhism belongs to this category of teaching.

Shakyamuni taught the truth of the Dharma in many different ways, according to people's comprehension, abilities and temperament. The Pure Land path was his direct response to the pressing needs of ordinary men and women who hungered for a spiritual life without having to renounce the world or observe monastic precepts and taxing austerities. The masses needed a more accessible approach that presupposed neither extraordinary powers of meditation nor moral impeccability. In other words, a path that took full account of the weakness and frailty of human beings with all their confused thoughts, disordered emotions and harmful impulses such as anger, greed and folly. It was for such people that Shakyamuni delivered his teaching about Amida Buddha and the Pure Land.

In Mahayana Buddhism, it is taught that there is fundamentally one reality which, in its highest and purest dimension, is experienced as Nirvana. It is also known, as we have seen, as the Dharma-Body (considered as the ultimate form of Being) or 'Suchness' (*Tathata* in Sanskrit) when viewed as the essence of all things. Another way to look at it is to regard the Dharma-Body as the highest reality and Nirvana as our experience of it.

> The Dharma-Body is eternity, bliss, true self and purity. It is forever free of all birth, ageing, sickness and death.
>
> —*Nirvana Sutra*

Infinite Light

The Dharma-Body is the immaterial foundation of all existence: from the most sublime spiritual states to the coarsest level of matter. Everything in the universe—all forms and all energy—is a manifestation of this deeper, hidden reality beyond space and time. As rays of light shine from the sun, while remaining undivided from their source, so the world flows forth from the Infinite which, because it is limitless, also lies at the heart of all things. Unlike the concept of God in some theistic religions, the Dharma-Body is not an all-powerful, interventionist deity remote from its creation; neither does it 'will' the world into existence through divine decree. The universe is simply a spontaneous disclosure of the boundless force that constitutes the eternal Dharma-Body. It is in its very nature—as infinite reality—to pour itself out ceaselessly in this way.

> The Dharma-Body, being formless, takes on all forms.
>
> — Seng-chao

However, in its beginningless unfolding as the totality of the universe and everything in it, it assumes forms that are limited, fragmented and, therefore, imperfect. In other words, the Dharma-Body expresses itself in appearances which, while ultimately inseparable from it (seeing as there is only one reality), are nevertheless finite and, as such, subject to decay and passing away. Furthermore, as these expressions are countless in number, they must also encompass possibilities that are negative from our point of view. The Dharma-Body is not omnipotent; therefore, it cannot remove the suffering, imperfection and flaws that are inherent in conditioned existence (such as physical pain and disease, not to mention the appalling evils of which deeply damaged people are capable).

Consider the full moon on a clear night and how it reflects its image. Sometimes it appears serene as on the surface of a calm lake. At other times, on a muddy pond, it is murky; or dynamic and ever-changing in its reflection over a fast-flowing river. Each of these varied and momentary images is clearly not to be confused with the abiding presence of the moon itself but, on the other hand, neither can they be seen as completely separate from it. While all metaphors have their limitations, this might be a helpful way of understanding the subtle and complex relationship between infinite reality and the finite world around us.

> The Dharma-Body, though manifesting itself in the world, is free from impurities and desires. It unfolds itself here, there and everywhere responding to the call of karma. It is not an individual reality or a false existence but is universal and pure. It comes from nowhere and it goes to nowhere; it does not assert itself nor is it subject to annihilation. It is forever serene and eternal. It is the One, devoid of all determinations. This body of Dharma has no boundary and no quarters but is embodied in all bodies. Its freedom or spontaneity is incomprehensible as is its spiritual presence in things corporeal. Assuming any concrete material form as required by the nature and condition of karma, it illuminates all creations. There is no place in the universe where this Body does not prevail. The universe becomes but this Body forever remains. It is free from all opposites and contraries, yet is working in all things to lead them to Nirvana.
>
> — *Flower Garland Sutra*

As human beings, we suffer because our deepest self is essentially one with the Dharma-Body (which, unbeknownst to us, we are seeking all the time) and yet, in our ignorance, we look for it in those things that are but its ephemeral appearances. This is why we are so constantly disappointed by the shortcomings of everything we encounter and pursue. It is as if we recognise something of this higher reality glittering in our world of forms but, when we aim to grasp it, it dissipates like gossamer in the wind. This is what constitutes the tragedy of our human condition. We are made for the Infinite, yet we are utterly absorbed in the things of this world, believing that what we are really looking for can be found in the midst of our routine life. Such a life, however, is but a distant reflection of this reality wherein lies our true sanctuary.

> Just as there are no material forms outside space, so there are no beings outside the Dharma-Body. —Vasubandhu

Not only is this reality all that truly exists (despite the tendency of our minds to fragment experience into irreducible subjects and objects) but it is also the font of all that is good, beautiful and true in the world. From the side of this reality, there is no separation between it and us but, from where we stand, the distance appears unbridgeable—and yet, in those rare moments where we experience profound joy in our lives, we are, in fact, making contact with traces or echoes of Nirvana in the world.

As difficult as it may be to grasp, the eternal world of the Dharma-Body and the transitory world of ordinary existence are one in essence and so the former cannot but disclose itself through the latter. We are able to see evidence of this all around us despite the darkness that can envelop our lives. In fact, our very world would not be possible unless it had its foundation in an absolute reality without which we should not expect anything to exist at all.

> The Mind in terms of the Absolute is the one world of Reality and the essence of all phases of existence in their totality.
> —*Awakening of Faith in the Mahayana*

According to the Mahayana teaching, the ultimate reality is formless and inconceivable. Therefore, it is impossible—from our limited perspective—to know it as it is in itself, since it surpasses all our sense perceptions and ordinary faculties of knowledge.

> The Dharma-Body . . . has neither colour nor form; thus, the mind cannot grasp it nor words describe it. —Shinran

While we may be able to surmise something of its existence

through our intuitive apprehension of its manifested qualities in the world, we cannot know anything about its true nature unless that same reality divulges itself to us in some way. All the teachings conveyed to us are but the Dharma-Body revealing itself through the agency of the historical Buddha. The fundamental truth we discover through Shakyamuni's teachings is that this reality is the highest wisdom and compassion, and that it seeks to bring us to the 'Pure Land'—the illimitable sphere of Nirvana.

> The Buddha-land, like the realm of unconditioned Nirvana,
> is pure and serene, resplendent and blissful.
> —*Sutra on the Buddha of Infinite Life*

> The land of bliss is the realm of Nirvana, the uncreated. . . .
> Undefiled by passions, unarisen, it is true reality.
> —Shan-tao

And so we come to the Pure Land tradition. Unlike other schools of Buddhism, which have given greater prominence to abstruse philosophies, demanding meditations and complex rituals, Shakyamuni also revealed a way that lay people could comprehend and practise in their lives. In order, then, to bring the formidable heights of Nirvana down to earth, he devised an expedient approach to capture our imagination through the deployment of striking images, aimed at rousing our aspiration for enlightenment.

The renowned Buddhist thinker, D.T. Suzuki, once said: 'The highest reality is not a mere abstraction; it is very much alive with sense and intelligence and, above all, with love purged of human infirmities and defilements'. It is this aspect of the Dharma-Body that is given special emphasis in the Pure Land tradition, which is dedicated to the spiritual needs of the 'person in the street'. In fact, the unfathomable compassion directed by this reality towards us is so great that the requirements on the individual—by way of practice—are reduced to simply surrendering to it. We will explore this feature of the teaching further in the next chapter.

In order to convey the compassionate nature of this reality and its unconditional embrace of all beings, Shakyamuni relates a compelling story. In the *Sutra on the Buddha of Infinite Life*, he tells us about a king who, on hearing the teachings of the Buddha of his time, 'rejoiced in his heart and awakened aspiration for the highest, perfect Enlightenment'. Earnestly seeking to save the multitude of suffering beings, 'he renounced his kingdom and throne, and became a monk called Dharmakara. Having superior intelligence, courage and wisdom, he distinguished himself in the world.'

Dharmakara then became a bodhisattva (a being devoted to pursuing enlightenment for themselves and others) and sought guidance from the Buddha of his time about how he could become a Buddha himself and establish a supra-mundane realm in order 'to save living beings from birth-and-death and lead them all to emancipation'. He goes on to say:

> When I have become a Buddha, my land shall be most exquisite, and its people wonderful and unexcelled;
> My land, being like Nirvana itself, shall be beyond compare.
> I take pity on living beings and resolve to save them all. . . .
> [They] shall find joy and serenity of heart;
> When they reach my land, they shall dwell in peace and happiness.

Thus resolved, Dharmakara made forty-eight specific vows to give effect to his noble aspiration and then proceeded, by dint of difficult and selfless practices, over many lifetimes, to realise his intention of 'producing a glorious and exquisite land'. In pursuing his path to enlightenment,

> He did not harbour any thought of greed, hatred or cruelty; nor did he allow any ideas of greed, hatred or cruelty to arise. He was unattached to any form, sound, smell, taste,

> touch or idea. Possessed of the power to persevere, he did not avoid undergoing various afflictions. Having little desire for his own sake, he knew contentment. Without any impure thought, enmity or stupidity, he dwelt continually in tranquil meditation. His wisdom was unobstructable, and his mind free of falsehood and deceitfulness. With an expression of tenderness in his face and with kindness in his speech, he spoke to others in consonance with their inner thoughts. Courageous and diligent, strong-willed and untiring, he devoted himself solely to the pursuit of the Dharma, thereby benefiting a multitude of beings. During innumerable aeons, he adorned his practice with a great store of merit and amassed virtues. In so doing, he enabled sentient beings to partake of them.

We are told that Dharmakara eventually became a Buddha called 'Amida' and created a realm, by the name of 'Peace and Bliss', where all his vows for the benefit of beings were fulfilled. The sutra then aims to impart a sense of the blissfulness of this land by resorting to highly imaginary and fantastic symbolism.

> In that Buddha-land, the earth is composed of seven jewels[2]—namely, gold, silver, beryl, coral, amber, agate and ruby—which have appeared spontaneously. The land itself is so vast, spreading boundlessly to the farthest extent, that it is impossible to know its limit. All the rays of light from these jewels intermingle and create manifold creations, producing a dazzling illumination. Those pure, superb and exquisite adornments are unsurpassed in all the worlds of the ten quarters. . . .
>
> In that land, there are innumerable jewelled nets, all adorned with skeins of gold thread, pearls and a hundred thousand kinds of rare and marvellous treasures. All around these nets hang jewelled bells of the utmost beauty, which

2. Jewels represent the permanence and indestructibility of Nirvana in contrast to the mutable conditions of our world.

> shine brilliantly. When a natural breeze of virtue arises and gently blows, it is moderate in temperature, neither cold nor hot, refreshing and soft to the senses, and moves neither too slowly nor too quickly. When the breeze wafts over the nets and the various jewelled trees, countless excellent sounds of the Dharma are heard, and ten thousand kinds of delicate fragrances of virtue are diffused. If one smells those fragrances, one's impurities and passions spontaneously cease to arise. . . .

To the modern Western mind, dazzled by the achievements of science and tyrannised by rational thought, such descriptions must seem extravagant nonsense; the product of an over-active imagination engrossed in a bizarre fantasy world. However, such a judgement would be premature and, perhaps, a little lacking in imagination itself.

The story of Dharmakara typifies the way in which the ancient Indian mind sought to present spiritual truths—namely in images that were both mentally and emotionally arresting. They are not to be taken as a literal description of what Nirvana is like; neither are they describing a physical location in the universe billions of miles from earth. Rather, they are an attempt to embody an ineffable mystery: to suggest, through reference to experiences that we value in our world, something of the splendour of Nirvana which can never adequately be captured in words.

> When I consider the features of that world, I see that . . . it is infinite, like space, vast and boundless. —Vasubandhu

We are creatures bound by language and, when ordinary words inevitably fail us as we try to describe the indescribable, we must have recourse to words and images that are out of the ordinary, which force us to suspend the banal and habitual thinking that dominates our lives, so that we are jolted into a radically new way of seeing things.

In the same way, we cannot consider the story of Dharmakara as an event that actually took place in what we regard as conventional historic time. However, that is not to say that the spiritual facts revealed by the sutra are not true. Dharmakara's vows represent the fundamental desire of ultimate reality to deliver us from ignorance and suffering. From another perspective, Dharmakara is also, in essence, 'us' in the aspect of our true or universal self. What he vowed for all sentient beings – their ultimate happiness and liberation—is what our principal desire would be too, were it not for the heavy cloak of nescience that conceals our intrinsic identity with all living things through the unity we share in the Dharma-Body.

In talking about the story of Dharmakara, one is very reluctant to use the word 'myth' because modern people associate it with something that is false when, in fact, myths the world over are imbued with deep truths about the human condition and its relationship to the transcendent. They do not have to be historical in order to be true. In any case, the 'facts' of history are themselves often elusive and amenable to conflicting interpretations.

The power of myth and symbolism lies in its ability to address us at a primal level of our being and to speak to archetypal realities that have always been at the core of human life. Such insights transcend history in that they do not depend on any particular events for their authority. They speak to us directly and we are able to recognise their truth through our faculties of intuition and spiritual awareness—even through our imagination which is also a vehicle for conveying truth, despite the superficial prejudice that it belongs to the world of make-believe. Music and poetry, too, possess this power to go beyond rational thought and provoke a holistic vision of our existence.

Recalling the earlier observation that the highest reality is pervaded by a purified intelligence and love, we come to see that it must also possess personality—not in the sense of an ordinary human being but in a manner that is without limitations or deficiencies. It is supra-personal in that it is more than we understand a person to be, but in no way impersonal; it is the source of all personality without those aspects that are prone to passion or delusion. In other words, it is a pure personality free of imperfections.

This is how Shin Buddhism envisages Amida Buddha - the direct expression of the formless Dharma-Body that has taken the initiative in response to our existential distress and assumed the form of the Buddha of Infinite Light and Eternal Life.

Any talk of Amida Buddha and the Pure Land will inevitably provoke the retort that this is just another way of clinging to a belief in God and Heaven, which Buddhism purportedly denies. However, it is important to understand—as we have already said—that these realities are not fundamentally disparate; they are but different ways of viewing the Absolute. Amida is the personal aspect of this reality; the Buddha of Great Compassion who vows to assuage our inner travail.

The Pure Land, on the other hand, is the aspect of Nirvana representing 'Utmost Peace and Bliss' as we find described in the sutra. This is not a realm distant from our world; it is an active force that is deeply connected to our lives and which is constantly seeking to wake us from our spiritual torpor.

> [The Pure Land] is vast in extent, unsurpassed and supremely wonderful, always present and subject neither to decay nor change. —*Sutra on the Buddha of Infinite Life*

An important attribute in the Buddhist notion of the highest reality is that it comprises the essence of all things (including ourselves) which are none other than its unique but fleeting images. In this way, we are connected to everything as we have the same source in the Dharma-Body, which unites all existence and in which every being has its origin. Amida Buddha and the Pure Land represent the enlightened and purified dimension of this reality whereas the impermanence, imperfection and suffering we experience represent the limitations that arise when the Dharma-Body emerges from itself to take on the infinite forms of conditioned life. This is something that it does naturally, without any design or calculation, in the way that fire radiates heat or a flower yields its scent.

Despite the distance that we commonly feel from this reality, it is nevertheless present in us as our deepest self. While Buddhism refutes the notion of a fixed self or 'soul', it is the temporary self—our human ego and the short-lived body with all its passions—to which it refers. In fact, it does not actually deny this self at all. It simply sees it as a very fluid, inconstant, dream-like entity with no enduring reality. It cannot be relied on to provide us with any lasting satisfaction and should not, therefore, be an object of attachment to us.

However, this is not to say that Buddhism teaches that any notion of self is mistaken—just that we usually look for our true self in the wrong place. In contrast to our individual ego, Buddhism points us towards the 'Great Self' which is the presence of the Dharma-Body in all of us, also known as *Buddha-nature.*

> Nirvana is called extinction of passions, the uncreated, peaceful happiness, eternal bliss, true reality, Dharma-Body . . . Suchness, Oneness and Buddha-nature . . . it fills the hearts and minds of the ocean of all beings. —Shinran

Without the presence of Buddha-nature in all things, it would be impossible for us to recognise the Buddha's wisdom when we encounter it. This wisdom, which is represented as *Light,* allows us to see things as they really are. Our Buddha-nature also lies behind our spiritual quest. It constitutes the powerful drive we feel to vanquish our darkness of mind and seek enlightenment.

Infinite Light

> Although I too am within Amida's grasp, blind passions obstruct my eyes and I cannot see the light; nevertheless, great compassion untiringly and constantly illumines me.
> —Genshin

The urge to attain spiritual wisdom has no other explanation than the activity of the Dharma-Body itself, which is ever aiming to lead us back to it. However, we should not harbour any illusions: that the Buddha-nature dwells in all beings is no reason to suppose that we are somehow already enlightened. Far from it. While its presence ensures that we can eventually overcome our benighted state, we remain ordinary people burdened by our shortcomings until such time as we realise Nirvana completely, at the end of our lives.

> When foolish beings possessed of blind passions attain birth in the Pure Land, they are no longer bound by karmic fetters. . . . That is, without severing blind passions, they realise Nirvana. —Shinran

Harking back to our discussion in the previous chapter, we may slowly begin to see how it is that we spend so much of our day-to-day existence running after shadows. As it forms our very substance, nothing less than the Infinite can satisfy us. Indeed, our ardent attachment to life itself is but a reflection of our desire for the Infinite, alienation from which accounts for our constant state of dissatisfaction. All desires, in fact, even ones that appear aberrant or abnormal, are rooted in the quest for consummate fulfilment and the need to be humanly complete. However, true wholeness of being is bound to remain wanting as long as our lives lack the sustenance of Amida Buddha's light which lies at the heart of even all our earthly joys.

> If sentient beings encounter the Buddha's light, their defilements are removed; they feel tenderness, joy and pleasure, and good thoughts arise. If sentient beings in the realm of

> suffering see this light, they will be relieved and freed from affliction. At the end of their lives, they all reach emancipation. —*Sutra on the Buddha of Infinite Life*

Without the existence of that which is timeless to which we can aspire for genuine liberation from all that is transient, any so-called spiritual path would remain meaningless and ineffectual. Despite the prevalent view held by many in the West, Buddhism is not a secular or humanistic philosophy, nor merely a 'rational' religion. It is a religion in the true sense of the word (from the Latin, *religare*, 'to bind') in that it binds us to authentic reality.

> The light of wisdom exceeds all measure,
> And every finite living being
> Receives this illumination that is like the dawn,
> So take refuge in Amida, the true and real light.
> —Shinran

In speaking this way, we must take care to avoid misleading anthropomorphic views of ultimate reality, which resists the ascription of any human attributes. Our limited intellects cannot fathom this measureless realm but we can experience it. Inconceivable does not imply unknowable, especially when this reality makes the approach towards us assuming a host of compassionate guises that are suited to our understanding and our needs.

By revealing itself as Infinite Light and Eternal Life, the Dharma-Body has sought to convey to us not only a sense of what it is but, more tangibly, to proclaim the unconditional nature of Amida Buddha's clasp of all beings.

> The light of compassion illumines us from afar;
> Those beings it reaches, it is taught,
> Attain the joy of dharma,
> So take refuge in Amida, the great consolation.
> —Shinran

The modern world demands that we remain sceptical and incredulous about such claims, which it insists are irrational fodder for the weak-minded. However, critics fail to see the serious limitations of rational thought which can only be helpful if it has adequate raw material with which to work. If our premises are bereft of wisdom, then the foundation of any argument we base on them will be barren.

Logic helps us to think clearly and to make proper inferences but its value is restricted if the basis of our deductions is impoverished to start with. Mere logic and rationality cannot create meaning. The essence of everything we value in life goes far beyond the mind that analyses and dissects; such a mind does not inspire or nourish the spirit.

Therefore, we need to reconsider our frequently uncritical attitude to what constitutes evidence. Spiritual truths are not amenable to scientific analysis, as they are not discrete components of our material world. They cannot be swept away for the mere reason that logic or science cannot grasp them. Our rational minds are certainly free to draw conclusions based on their experience but these would be of greater value if they did not restrict themselves solely to the raw data supplied by our senses, which can never give a complete account of reality.

Reflecting on these matters with an open mind, we come to have a forceful intuition of the non-material origin of all things. The very fact of consciousness points to the compelling argument that 'the greater cannot derive from the lesser'; in other words, the astonishing nature of the human mind and its extraordinary capacity (including, most significantly, the ability to question itself and the meaning of existence) is, surely, not something that anyone would attribute to the merely random permutation of sub-atomic particles which are, according to most scientists anyway, bereft of sentience altogether.

In fact, Mahayana Buddhism teaches that everything—including what we rather abstractly call 'matter'—is a manifestation of the Dharma-Body's supreme consciousness and therefore very much alive in its own way. All phenomena—from galaxies to mountains, rivers and trees—are emanations of one universal and all-pervading intelligence that reveals itself on limitless levels through innumerable forms, including the spectacular diversity of our natural and human worlds.

CHAPTER THREE

Awakening to the Real

We who aspire for Amida's land,
Though we differ in outward condition and conduct,
Should truly receive the Name of the Primal Vow
And never forget it, whether waking or sleeping.

—*Shinran*

Awakening to the Real

To many people in the West, Buddhism is simply a tradition based on the strict practice of meditation. This belief is held to such an extent that anyone who professes to be a Buddhist but does not meditate, in a formal sense, is summarily dismissed as an impostor. This is a serious misconception.

The very great majority of lay people living in Buddhist countries today do not meditate as a matter of course and few would even think to question their sincerity. We need to accept that the scope of Buddhist practice is very broad, encompassing numerous approaches to the goal of spiritual realisation and reflecting the immense variety we find in the aptitude and disposition of people.

The other difficulty is that many of those interested in Buddhism may not be very clear about what they mean by 'meditation' or what they hope to gain from it. The traditional objective of meditation is to realise the highest principle of existence through the concentrated application of both mind and body - it is not merely a technique for relaxation or stress relief. Therefore, it must sound almost heretical to suggest that meditation is not central (or even necessary) to authentic Buddhist practice but, in fact, this is the norm around the world wherever you find lay Buddhist communities: from Sri Lanka to Mongolia, from Cambodia to Korea, and from Laos to Japan.

The tradition of meditation is certainly important and features prominently among those who have entered monastic life to devote themselves exclusively to such practice and, of course, to those lay people who have also taken it up. However, we must firmly reject the Western prejudice that those who do not meditate methodically are second-class Buddhists bereft of a deeper experience or understanding of the teachings.

Another misconception is that only by practising 'good deeds' can one be a *bona fide* Buddhist, as if that was all there was to it. Following the Buddha's guidance on how to behave is certainly necessary in maintaining our moral equilibrium and in making our relations with others more harmonious, but it is not an end in itself. The Dharma is about awakening to the truth of existence, nothing less. Nowhere, in any Buddhist school, is it taught that enlightenment is brought about by merely observing rules of conduct.

Shin Buddhism belongs to the family of Pure Land schools that do not advocate meditation as the primary or most important form of Buddhist practice. To be sure, there are certainly well-established Pure Land meditation techniques (as detailed, for example, in the *Sutra on the Visualisation of the Buddha of Infinite Life*) but, over time, ordinary Buddhist followers began to seek refuge in a different path. This has often been described—sometimes in a derogatory sense—as a Buddhism of 'faith' and therefore disparaged owing to its alleged similarity to the Christian understanding of this term, thus leading some to regard it as inauthentic.

However, this so-called 'Buddhism of Faith' goes back many centuries—indeed, to the time of Shakyamuni himself—and cannot be dismissed quite so readily. Furthermore, 'faith' in this context does not mean a blind, uncritical belief in things unproven on the basis of a higher authority. It is a realisation rooted in the direct experience of reality coupled with the qualities of joy, serenity, trust, confidence and wisdom (*prasada* in Sanskrit).

> Entrusting is the mind full of truth, reality and sincerity; the mind of ultimacy, accomplishment, reliance and reverence;

> the mind of discernment, distinctness, clarity and faithfulness; the mind of aspiration . . . and exultation; the mind of delight, joy, gladness and happiness; hence, it is completely untainted by the hindrance of doubt. —Shinran

Faith, in this sense, is a way of knowing and not just holding a set of beliefs without confirming them in one's experience. Shakyamuni himself cautioned us not to accept anything just on his, or anybody else's, authority but to verify for ourselves—to the extent that we can—the truth of what he was saying.

When we consider the etymological root of 'faith', we find that its meaning is derived from the Latin, *fidere*, 'to trust': not because we are commanded to but because it is the natural outcome of our experience in hearing and reflecting on the Dharma. We come to trust that it is the path to awakening as we, gradually, confirm the truth of the teaching along the way.

Nevertheless, the word 'faith' has so many pejorative and misleading connotations that it may be best to use the Buddhist term corresponding to the state of mind we are trying to convey, in order to explain it without fear of being misunderstood. In doing so, the differences between it and the traditional Western notion of faith should become clear.

In Shin Buddhism, the primary spiritual experience is known as *shinjin* (信 心) the literal meaning of which is 'believing' or 'entrusting' heart and mind. From the perspective of the Dharma, entrusting (or *prasanna* in Sanskrit) does not mean mere belief or the acceptance of doctrine without engagement. Furthermore, the first character can also represent the Sanskrit word *shraddha* which is associated, in Buddhist thought, with clarity. Shinjin, then, can be spoken of as 'clarity of mind'. Again, in the light of Shinran's experience and insight, it is also feasible to translate it as the 'true and real mind'.

What makes it true and real? It is the mind of Amida Buddha which arises within us and becomes inseparable from our painful passions. On one level, of course, the two are diametrically opposed; our minds express confusion and insincerity, while that of the Buddha represents truth and light.

And yet, from Amida's perspective—which sees no opposition — they are embraced as one. The experience of shinjin is a paradox. On the one hand, we feel deep joy in finding ourselves bathed in the light of Amida Buddha and encountering true reality:

> Pure light, joyful light, the light of wisdom,
> Light constant, inconceivable, light beyond speaking,
> Light excelling the sun and moon he sends forth, illumining countless worlds; The multitude of beings all receive this radiance. —Shinran

This is a critical experience and marks a permanent transformation in our lives. On the other hand, we are made to see, through the long shadow cast by this light's sheer intensity, that:

> We should not express outwardly signs of wisdom, goodness or diligence, for inwardly we are possessed of falsity. We are filled with all manner of greed, anger, perversity, deceit, wickedness and cunning, and it is difficult to put an end to our evil nature. In this, we are like poisonous snakes or scorpions. —Shan-tao

Such a confronting insight can only be obtained through seeing ourselves, as we really are, through the eyes of Amida Buddha. Even those who possess some measure of genuine self-awareness, despite renouncing any kind of religious adherence, also reflect—in their own way—Amida's working which seeks to bring all beings to a knowledge of their false self and its perils.

How, then, is shinjin to be realised? How do we encounter the light that represents the wisdom of Amida Buddha? What are we required to do? Before we proceed to answer these questions, we need to examine the nature of practice. In Shin Buddhism, the notion of practice is tied up with its view of the mundane self. A problem arises when we try to overcome the limitations of the self-centred ego through practices that rely on this very self 'doing something' in order to escape its entrapment. A well-known metaphor is the idea of trying to pick yourself up by your own boot straps.

Shinran's great insight was that we cannot conquer the self by the self. Some kind of external agency is required: (a) to help us shed light on our ego as it really is in all its petty and baneful guises; and (b) to enable us to subdue the small 'self' with a view to realising the Great Self by awakening to Amida's light. Our ego cannot possibly accomplish this by relying on its own meagre resources without reaching an impasse. Furthermore, it is extremely reluctant to do so; it cannot and will not execute its own death warrant.

Clearly, a balanced ego and a healthy self-identity is essential to functioning properly in the world. However, it would be true to say that, generally speaking, our sense of self has a tendency to be closed in, separate and remote from others.

In Mahayana thought, all things are interconnected as they comprise different aspects of the one Dharma-Body. Therefore, the mistaken belief that what we perceive as external reality lies completely outside ourselves can be damaging to our psyche. The solution, according to Shinran, was to yield that to which we are most attached—our very self—to another power (*tariki* in Japanese, meaning 'Power of the Other'), this being Amida Buddha.

When we surrender ourselves in this way, we begin to experience intense relief from our tragic spiritual desolation and the crushing wretchedness that we have carried with us for so long.

This then compels us, naturally, to want to reject any practices that are tainted by the ineffectual 'power of the self' (*jiriki*)—we come to see them as impotent efforts based on the tenuous reality of the ego, which can only lead us down blind alleys.

Such practices include meditation when it is undertaken with a view to 'getting' enlightenment or practicing good deeds in the hope of acquiring 'merit'. These are all infected by a very subtle attitude of self-gain and the belief that more practice leads to better prospects for spiritual progress. However, this is a hopeless snare:

> Firmly setting our minds and undertaking practice in this way—even if we strive to the utmost with body and mind through the twelve periods of the day and night, urgently seeking and urgently acting as though sweeping fire from our heads—must all be called poisoned 'good' acts.
>
> —Shan-tao

Such a stark insight can only arise from an 'objective' view of the self that we gain when the light of Amida Buddha shines into the dark recesses of our hearts. This is an important dimension to our realisation of shinjin and a necessary one if we are to discover the truth about ourselves. It is a recognition that we are ordinary human beings afflicted with 'blind passion'. The scholars responsible for translating the *Collected Works of Shinran* offer the following observation:

> 'Blind passion' (*bonno*) is a comprehensive term descriptive of all the forces, conscious and unconscious, that propel the unenlightened person to think, feel, act and speak—whether in happiness or sorrow—in such a way as to cause uneasiness, frustration, torment and pain (mentally, emotionally, spiritually and even physically) for themselves and others. While Buddhism makes a detailed and subtle analysis of blind passion, employing such terms as craving, anger, delusion, arrogance, doubt and wrong views, fundamentally

> it is rooted in the fierce, stubborn clinging to the foolish and evil self that constitutes the basis of our existence. When we realise the full implications of this truth about ourselves, we see that the human condition is itself nothing but blind passion. Thus, just to live, or wanting to live, as an unenlightened being is to manifest blind passion at all times, regardless of what we may appear to be. One comes to know this, however, only through the illumination of great compassion. Hence, awakening to one's own nature is called 'the wisdom of shinjin' and the person who realises it has already been grasped by the Primal Vow.

They also say:

> It should be noted that, while the term 'evil' has moral and ethical implications in Shin Buddhism, its chief significance is religious. The essential meaning of the term 'evil' is a person's inability to perform any religious practice whatever—any act to bring about him or herself to the attainment of Buddhahood—because of the deeply harboured blind passions that motivate all their acts.

So what exactly is Amida Buddha's 'Primal Vow'? In the second chapter, we related the story of Dharmakara and how he strove to save all beings from suffering. The story goes on to say that his vows were fulfilled and that Dharmakara attained enlightenment, becoming Amida Buddha and establishing the Pure Land. These vows tangibly represent the great compassionate force at the heart of reality that seeks to liberate us from our spiritual bondage. The most important of these vows is the Eighteenth or 'Primal Vow' on which the entire Pure Land tradition rests. In the *Sutra on the Buddha of Infinite Life*, this vow is proclaimed as follows:

> If, when I attain Buddhahood, sentient beings in the lands of the ten quarters who sincerely and joyfully entrust themselves to me, desire to be born in my land and call my Name even ten times, should not be born there, may I not attain

> perfect Enlightenment. Excluded, however, are those who commit the five grave offences and abuse the right dharma.[3]

Central to this vow is the notion of entrusting to Amida Buddha which arises through our 'deep hearing' (*monpo*) of the Dharma. Entrusting means leaving our spiritual destiny to 'Other-Power' and rejecting any suggestion that we are capable of bringing about our own enlightenment through 'self-power' or 'poisoned' practices.

> Self-power . . . is endeavouring to make yourself worthy through mending the confusion in your acts, words and thoughts, confident of your own powers and guided by your own calculation. —Shinran

Although we speak of 'self' and 'other' power, there is—in truth—only the power of the Buddha which our specious pride appropriates for itself, thinking it can take credit for all our virtues and accomplishments.

Amida's light pervades all things so, in entrusting ourselves to

3. 'The last part of the 18th Vow has a special significance in Shinran's teaching. It is the only one among Amida's 48 Vows to possess such a clause of exclusion. In other words, the Vow that proclaims the universal enlightenment of all beings also includes the most stringent restriction. Shinran understands this clause as an expression of compassion so boundless and profound that it directs itself to the very person whom it censures – the being who has committed the five grave offences and slandered the dharma' (*The Collected Works of Shinran*, p.181). In the Mahayana, the five grave offences are: (1) destroying stupas, temples, sutras and Buddhist images; (2) slandering Buddhist disciples or the Mahayana teaching; (3) harassing the practice of a monk or causing his death; (4) killing one's father or mother, causing blood to flow from the body of the Buddha and disrupting the harmony of the sangha; and (5) committing the ten transgressions with the conviction that there will be no karmic recompense and without fear for the next life. The 'ten transgressions' are: killing, stealing, lying, being licentious, speaking harshly, divisively or idly, greed, anger and holding erroneous views.

it, we allow it to ferry us towards Nirvana, like a steady ship on a stormy ocean.

> We lack both the observance of precepts and the comprehension of wisdom, but when, by allowing ourselves to be carried on the ship of Amida's Vow, we have crossed this ocean of suffering that is birth-and-death and attain the shore of the Pure Land, the dark clouds of blind passion will swiftly clear and the moon of enlightenment, true reality, will immediately appear. Becoming one with the unhindered light filling the ten quarters, we will benefit all sentient beings. It is at that moment that we attain enlightenment.
> —*A Record in Lament of Divergences*

The notion of merely entrusting ourselves to Amida Buddha—which is central to the experience of shinjin—will strike some as being far too simple. Somehow, it does not seem quite enough; surely we should be doing more. We ought not to be deceived by this apparent simplicity. True entrusting is grounded in the working of the Buddha. It arises naturally (though not without considerable struggle and resistance at first) when we begin to see the truth of our dissembling ego in the untainted mirror of Amida's wisdom. Getting to this point, however, is not easy and requires great courage and honesty, as well as a willingness to take a risk in letting go of our stubborn self-attachment.

> 'To abandon the mind of self-power' is an admonishment to abandon the conviction that one is good, to cease relying on the self; to stop reflecting knowingly on one's evil heart and, further, to abandon the judging of people as good and bad.
> —Shinran

Entrusting that has its basis solely in our own will and striving will surely falter. According to Shinran, even our ability to fulfill the requirements of the Primal Vow ('sincere and joyful trust') has its source in Amida Buddha. The font of all real virtue lies in 'no-self' (from our point of view) or 'true self' (from the Buddha's aspect).

Genuine practice must have its genesis beyond ourselves; in any case, from the Mahayana perspective of non-duality, there can be no such thing as an independent or self-sufficient practicer. That is why, in Shin Buddhism, conventional practices are seen as ineffective if they are motivated by the conviction that, through them, we can eradicate our blind passions. This is impossible as long as we remain ordinary people with our intractable faults and weaknesses.

Shakyamuni urged us to examine ourselves and said that, if we looked deeply enough, we can find nothing stable, secure or permanent in our physical, mental or emotional constitution. What are we able to pin down as our real self? Our body? Our emotions? Our intellect? Our memories? These are constantly changing, always vacillating and never remaining the same from day to day. Attempts to find a distinct and enduring individual essence invariably flounder. Hence, we are urged by Shakyamuni to renounce such a self and take refuge in the sole reality of the Infinite, which we find embodied in the wisdom and compassion of Amida Buddha.

> Although sentient beings are impermanent, still their Buddha-nature is eternal and unchanging. —*Nirvana Sutra*

Shinjin is also *prajna* or wisdom as imparted to us by the Buddha but not merely what we consider to be so in a worldly sense. Indeed, Shinran explicitly states that 'great shinjin is itself Buddha-nature' which gradually unfolds within us, despite the tenacious presence of our ego and its clamorous demands. This wisdom needs to be perceived directly—'tasted' even—not just with the head but also with one's heart.

Furthermore, shinjin is the desire to attain enlightenment for both oneself and others.

> Shinjin is the aspiration to bring all beings to the attainment of supreme Nirvana; it is the heart of great love and compassion. —Shinran

When the wisdom of shinjin permeates our being, there can be no more compelling form of knowledge. Shinjin is also lively, dynamic and vibrant. It opens up new and rich possibilities for viewing the world and ourselves. In this sense, Shinran acknowledged that, for the person of shinjin, 'birth in the Pure Land' is not just a posthumous event. It also heralds the emergence, in this life, of the Buddha-mind within our own debased consciousness, leading to an expanded awareness of reality.

> When persons realise pure shinjin that is true and real, they realise the mind of great joy. Concerning the attainment of the mind of great joy, the Sutra states: 'The person who aspires with a sincere mind to be born in the land of happiness shall reach the full illumination of wisdom and acquire virtues unexcelled.' —Shinran

Therefore, the path to this goal will differ for each individual but the destination is the same: the awakening of shinjin here and now and the assurance of entering the ocean of Nirvana when we sunder our bonds to this world at the time of death.

> It is like the ocean's nature having one taste; when various streams enter, they necessarily become the one taste, and the ocean's taste does not alter. —T'an-luan

From the Buddhist point of view, suffering does not necessarily come to an end when we die. Depending on the karma generated in both this and previous lifetimes, we may well continue on a dismal course through various modes and levels of post-mortem existence until such time as we are freed from the doleful round of transmigration (*samsara*). This is not a didactic allegory concocted to make us behave better. Rather, it underscores a cardinal truth about reality and how it is formed by a chain of cause and effect that stretches back to an indeterminate past.

The Primal Vow seeks to end this cycle of aimless transmigration by bringing all beings to Nirvana through expunging the conditions that keep them trapped in the cycle. This can only happen when we allow the pure karma of Amida Buddha to 'overwhelm' our own, so to speak. Yet we must patiently see out our lives with the 'debt' we have incurred and brought into our present life, as well as reap the consequences of any unfavourable karma that we create during our time in this world.

> The light of purity is without compare.
> When a person encounters this light,
> All bonds of karma fall away;
> So take refuge in Amida, the ultimate shelter.
> —Shinran

Consider a potter spinning a wheel that keeps her pot constantly revolving. This is like the energy or force that we fuel with our unenlightened actions. The breaking through of Amida Buddha's light into our lives—in the form of shinjin—is like the potter suddenly taking her foot off the pedal of the spinning wheel. The momentum driving the motion of the pot then ceases but it must continue to spin a little longer until it comes to a complete rest. In this way, Amida breaches our spiritual husk to drain away the posthumous effects of any adverse karma we accrue subsequent to the arising of shinjin – karma that would otherwise continue to subject us to the yoke of transmigration indefinitely.

> Those who attain true and real shinjin . . . necessarily attain Nirvana. . . . To attain Nirvana is to attain eternal bliss. Eternal bliss is ultimate tranquility. —Shinran

Nevertheless, we must endure the rest of our lives saddled with our human imperfections, even though we may carry them much more lightly as we await our final state of liberation in the Pure Land.

> The beings born there have lofty and brilliant wisdom. They are all of one form, without any differences. . . . They are all endowed with bodies of Naturalness, Emptiness and Infinity. —*Sutra on the Buddha of Infinite Life*

So while we all have to struggle with the same challenges and difficulties that life throws at us, the crucial difference is that people of shinjin live their lives conscious of being bathed in the compassionate light of Amida Buddha while others may simply have to carry their existential burden alone, without any spiritual relief. The life of shinjin, however, is suffused with joy notwithstanding the various tribulations that we must bear in this world.

Amida Buddha does not judge or discriminate. All beings are embraced and will, eventually, attain emancipation.

> In reflecting on the great ocean of shinjin, I realise that there is no discrimination between noble and humble or black-robed monks and white-clothed laity, no differentiation between man and woman, old and young. The amount of evil one has committed is not considered; the duration of any performance of religious practices is of no concern. It is a matter of neither practice nor good acts . . . neither meditative practice nor non-meditative practice, neither right contemplation nor wrong contemplation . . . neither daily life nor the moment of death. It is simply serene faith that is inconceivable, inexplicable and indescribable. It is like the medicine that eradicates all poisons. The medicine of the Buddha's Vow destroys the poisons of our wisdom and our foolishness. —Shinran

Not everybody can be liberated at once as people are at different stages of spiritual development and maturity. Some in this life will never encounter Amida Buddha because of scepticism, doubt, indifference or even outright hostility and contempt for the sacred. However, they are never abandoned—indeed, Amida pursues them relentlessly until they succumb, as they must in the end, to the Buddha's merciful call which beckons us all to seek release from the chains of our spiritual thraldom.

Shinjin, therefore, is a form of enlightenment (indeed the highest possible for ordinary people) but it does not turn us into Buddhas in this life. Our lives may be steeped in Amida's light—which is a constant source of wonder—but we do not thereby become flawless individuals. We remain fully human with all the perils and anxieties that come with being mortal and yet our faith in the Infinite is able to sustain us through the vexing uncertainties of life. It allows us to live in the great realm of the spirit, which is not some distant or unattainable abstraction but a reality that dwells in the very midst of our everyday world.

> Sentient beings who are mindful of Amida Buddha are like persons who, imbued with incense, bear its fragrance on their bodies; hence, they are called 'those adorned with the fragrance of light'.
>
> —*Sutra on the Samadhi of Heroic Advance*

So while we may lament our condition and the harm we inflict on others and ourselves, as well as the pain we endure in turn, our lives are enriched with a lively and irresistible joy that stems from the presence of Amida Buddha's mind within us. This mind does not displace our own but, rather, both abide together, the one constantly illuminating the other.

In recognising that there is more to our existence than suffering and disappointment, we can awaken to a higher perspective from which we are able to integrate the effects of our perturbing worldly predicaments. Furthermore, a deeper appreciation of the impermanence of life and the illusory nature of our ego goes a long way towards blunting the impact of many a blow that could otherwise cause us deep consternation. We are not suggesting that our human responses to life's challenges are in any way diluted; indeed, they are fortified by the strength and courage we receive from having our lives firmly embedded in the security, certainty and serenity that comes with being embraced, just as we are, by Amida Buddha.

'Just as we are'—this is crucial. We are not expected to earn this gift from Amida. Neither are we required to become smarter or more virtuous in order to be worthy of it.

> Since we are possessed of blind passions, the Buddha receives us without judging whether our hearts are good or bad.
>
> —Shinran

The Primal Vow is such that it accepts ordinary people for what they are—foolish and fractious beings with no hope of saving themselves. It does not demand moral or intellectual qualifications. This is the meaning of unconditional compassion. All it asks is that we admit the Primal Vow into our lives and let it do its work of transforming our awareness.

> In the long night of ignorance, it is the torch:
> The wisdom-eye is in darkness, yet do not sorrow.
> In the vast sea of birth-and-death, it is the raft:
> The hindrance of evil karma weighs heavy, yet do not grieve.
>
> —Shinran

Some will retort that all this other-worldly talk of enlightenment and Nirvana is all very well but would we not be better off devoting ourselves to assisting others rather than being so preoccupied with our own deliverance? There is no conflict between the two. Of course, as moral beings we seek, however inadequately, to help our fellows and make the world a better place in which to live. We do not cease to function as social individuals just because we happen to have spiritual aspirations.

In fact, those whose lives have been touched by the light of Amida Buddha may well exhibit an increased sensitivity to suffering in the world and thereby be naturally inclined towards relieving it. Nevertheless,

> However much love and pity we may feel in this life, it is difficult to save others as we would wish; hence, such compassion remains unfulfilled. —Shinran

So even more important than material or emotional support to others (imperative as that it is while also subject to significant constraints) is sharing the Buddha's teaching with them so that a seed may be sown for their ultimate spiritual benefit, without which our lives would remain directionless.

Finally, we would like to address a very important doctrinal feature that first arose when we introduced the Primal Vow of Amida Buddha; that is, the reference to Amida's 'Name'. This notion forms the crux of Shin Buddhism's understanding of practice. The *raison d'être* of the Name in Pure Land thought perplexes many Westerners who are approaching it for the first time. Indeed, it can be very difficult to navigate the labyrinth of traditional doctrinal teachings on this subject, so let us try to state the matter as simply as we can.

In the previous chapter, we discussed the fact that the ultimate reality in Buddhism—the Dharma-Body—is formless, inconceivable and utterly beyond our comprehension. How is it, then, that we are able to establish any kind of contact with something so unapproachable? From where we stand, it must seem a kind of void; indeed, one of the words used in Mahayana Buddhism to describe it is *shunyata*, meaning 'void' or 'emptiness'. Not because it is nothing or non-existent but because it is 'empty' of that which is limited, finite or conditioned; in other words, unlike anything with which we are familiar in everyday life.

> Suchness is empty because, from the very beginning, it has never been related to any defiled states of existence; it is free from all marks of individual distinction and has nothing to do with thoughts conceived by a deluded mind.
> —*Awakening of Faith in the Mahayana*

Therefore, in order to become manifest, this reality must assume a form by which we can recognise it; otherwise, it would remain forever silent and unknown.

In Shin Buddhism, the Dharma-Body reveals itself to us not only in the forms of Amida Buddha and the Pure Land that we find in the sutras but also—more dynamically—as the Name 南無阿彌陀佛 (pronounced in Japanese as *Namo Amida Butsu*). This is a transliteration from the original Sanskrit, *Namo 'mitabhaya Buddhaya.* Indeed, Amida vowed that this Name would be the means through which we could come to know the Buddha and attain release from our spiritual fetters.

It is noteworthy that the Name is not simply 'Amida' or 'Amida Butsu' (*butsu* is Japanese for 'Buddha') but *Namo Amida Butsu.* What is the meaning of *Namo*? *Namo* (a variation of the Sanskrit *namas*) is the act of adoration, paying homage, taking refuge or relying on something. The Name, therefore, has two closely-related meanings. On the one hand, we are exhorted to depend on Amida Buddha exclusively: 'Take refuge in me'.

When we encounter the Name and slowly begin to unravel its significance (through study, self-reflection, meeting a good teacher and listening to the teachings), the truth of Amida's Primal Vow becomes real to us for the first time. This is called 'hearing the Name' which is, itself, the experience of shinjin where we awaken to true reality.

The establishment of shinjin involves an active quest on our part and is not just a matter of self-induced 'belief' or mere hope. There is a necessary process of seeking until shinjin becomes settled. This is consistent with the practice of Shakyamuni himself whereby he led his followers, one by one, to an awareness of the truth.

If we 'hear' deeply—not just with our ears but with our whole being—we will come to realise that the Primal Vow is directed to us personally in the midst of our agitated lives. Indeed, it is often in moments of dire crisis or distress that we may be able to hear this call most clearly.

> Because the power of the Vow is without limits,
> Even our evil karma, so deep and heavy is not burdensome,
> Because the Buddha's wisdom is without bounds,
> Even the bewildered and wayward are not abandoned.
>
> —Shinran

At the same time, we experience the other side of this realisation—the awareness that the Primal Vow takes us in 'warts and all', regardless of our transgressions and carries us to the Pure Land. Coming to this understanding leads to an outpouring of relief, joy and gratitude expressed in our invoking the Name—*Namo Amida Butsu*—with the meaning, in this case, 'I take refuge in Amida Buddha' in response to the Buddha's original call to us.

Namo Amida Butsu also signifies the fundamental unity of us (represented by *Namo*) and Amida (*Amida Butsu*). This is not the same as identity but, in saying the Name, the two become indissolubly united.

The invocation of Amida's Name as the direct expression of our shinjin is known as the *nembutsu.* Originally, this term meant contemplating, or the act of thinking on, the Buddha but, gradually, it also came to encompass recitation of the Name when undertaken in a state of faithful and entrusting mindfulness. The nembutsu, therefore, is the embodiment—the evident and discernible sign—of our shinjin. It is not a mantra to be used as a means for procuring spiritual benefits.

According to Shinran, as the realisation of shinjin is the awakening of Amida Buddha's mind within us, the nembutsu that is invoked with this awareness is, in fact, the action of Amida coursing through our very being and emerging as *Namo Amida Butsu* from our mouths. The nembutsu is thus the living voice of the Eternal Buddha declaring its presence in our world of suffering. Considered in this way, Amida becomes the impetus behind every genuine utterance of the Name. This is why Shinran states:

> Great Practice is to say the Name of the Buddha of Unhindered Light.

In other words, 'great practice' is not something that *we* do; it does not belong to us but to Amida Buddha. In the nembutsu that has its source in 'Other-Power', we come to receive Amida's virtues which infuse our mind and body with every invocation. This is how Amida Buddha transfers the spiritual energy of Nirvana to us and, with it, the force that propels us to the Pure Land.

> Amida Buddha grasps beings with the Name. Thus, as we hear it with our ears and say it with our lips, exalted virtues without limit grasp and pervade our hearts and minds. It becomes ever after the seed of our Buddhahood.
>
> —Shinran

In this respect, our reception of Amida's power is completely passive, for there is nothing we can add to it. The nembutsu becomes the vehicle through which Amida's presence fills our being with the light of wisdom and transfigures our personality.

Mere recitation of the nembutsu without the corresponding realisation of shinjin is fruitless because it has its basis in the wavering and unstable faith of the individual who continues to harbour doubt regarding the efficacy of the Primal Vow. However, even those who practise with an attitude of 'self-power' in the hope of attaining shinjin are also embraced by Amida. Many people start, tentatively, on the path through merely reciting the nembutsu, or trying to perform meditation or virtuous deeds, without any deep conviction or sense of Amida's presence.

Nevertheless, even these initial steps have their promptings in the compassionate working of Amida Buddha and therefore cannot simply be dismissed as mere 'self-power' actions. Such people may come to see, through the limitations they encounter in these practices, the Other-Power that sustains the experience of shinjin. In fact, any form of practice devoted towards enlightenment, be it sitting meditation, tantra, visualisation and so on, has the potential to become transmuted into an awareness of the Buddha's activity working through it.

Shinran's unique contribution to spiritual thought was the radical insight that true practice is something that is bestowed on us. Only the highest reality can undertake practice, so to speak, with the requisite level of purity and perfection. All that remains for us to do, therefore, is to recognise our inability to contribute anything to the working of Amida Buddha and to simply accept what is offered to us without conditions.

> Faith does not arise from within one's self;
> The entrusting heart is given by the Other-Power.
> —Rennyo

This may sound rather strange, or as if it is some kind of defection from 'standard' Buddhism, but it is a perfectly logical conclusion from the basic Buddhist premise regarding the inherently precarious and dream-like nature of the conventional self. In Shin Buddhism, it is understood that, from this self, nothing conducive to genuine enlightenment can possibly emerge.

Therefore, despite the widespread misconception, it is simply not true that Shin Buddhism ignores practice. On the contrary, it demands that practice be completely devoid of human weakness and delusion to be fully effective. The only way that this condition can be met is if we accept—in utter humility—that we are truly incapable of union with the Infinite so long as we depend on our paltry abilities, which are clearly incommensurate with such a goal.

We must completely surrender to the true practice given through the nembutsu by which Amida Buddha's all-pervading wisdom and compassion is imparted to us. Once we can honestly accept this state of affairs as our only option—in view of the bleak realities of our human plight—our response can only be the natural and spontaneous utterance of the nembutsu in joyous recognition of our ultimate destiny.

> The sacred name of Amida surpasses measure, description and conceptual understanding; it is the Name of the Vow embodying great love and great compassion, which brings all sentient beings into the supreme Nirvana . . . the Name spreads universally throughout the worlds in the ten quarters and guides all to the practice of the Buddha's teaching.
>
> —Shinran

The nembutsu is the 'endowed practice' of Amida Buddha that is unceasingly directed to us and in which we can seek refuge at any time. Often, the nembutsu comes unbidden to us in moments of either exultation or despair. It is Amida's declaration, 'I am always with you'. This gives us the confidence, resolve and tenacity to endure misfortune and disappointment in our lives. The light of the Buddha provides the foundation for a life of freedom: freedom from habitually corrosive emotions, freedom from debilitating self-absorption, freedom from oppressive guilt, freedom from the trauma of our broken lives, and freedom to live, right now, in a higher realm that can nourish and enliven our existence.

> Do not meaninglessly despise yourself, weaken your heart, and doubt the Buddha's wisdom, which surpasses conceptual understanding. . . . The mind of trust alone is essential. There is no need to consider anything else.
>
> —Shinran

The charge that Shin Buddhism ignores meditation and is therefore disqualified from being a proper Buddhist path warrants a response. If, by meditation, we mean a formal course of prescribed practices designed to eliminate our negative states of mind so that we can attain a faultless personality and overcome our human shortcomings then, no, Shin Buddhists do not meditate as they reject the very premise that practices based on self-centred actions can ever negate the self. Indeed, pursuing the much-coveted objective of enlightenment on such terms is considered impossible, if not harmful.

If, on the other hand, we take meditation to mean cultivating extraordinary powers of concentration that enable us to experience (albeit fleetingly) sublime transcendental states of selflessness then, again no, Shin followers do not observe such practices either because these super-human feats are beyond them or, more importantly, considered useless in improving the quality of our spiritual life. Such esoteric pursuits can often lead to an unhealthy degree of competitiveness among practitioners that ill-behoves their Buddhist beliefs regarding the wiles and subterfuges of the ego.

However, if we are asked: Is Shin Buddhism a contemplative path, meaning a state of natural mindfulness of Amida Buddha where we are led to a lively and expansive awareness, dwelling in a joyful faith that touches eternity, coupled with a strong desire to share this realisation with others, then the answer must be: 'Undoubtedly'. This is a meditation of sorts, perhaps, but it is blithe, carefree, buoyant and invigorating; not a means to an end. It is none other than the unhindered expression of a life immersed in the splendour of Amida's infinite light.

CHAPTER FOUR

Joy Amidst the Shadows

The light of compassion illumines us always and the darkness of our ignorance is already broken through. Yet the clouds and mists of greed, desire, anger and hatred always obscure the sky of true faith. But though the light of the sun is veiled by clouds and mists, below them there is still brightness. —*Shinran*

Joy Amidst the Shadows

We now turn to the more practical dimensions of Shin Buddhism in everyday life, by which we mean to suggest how some of the issues raised in this book may have broader application in areas such as morality, our emotional life and the experience of beauty.

Let us commence with a consideration of morals. The first thing that must be stressed is that Shin is certainly not indifferent to ethical concerns, despite claims regarding its unfavourable view of human nature. Like all Buddhists, Shin followers treasure Shakyamuni's teachings as handed down in the Four Noble Truths, the Eight-fold Path and the Six Perfections. [4] They also endeavour, like all sincere Buddhists, to live by these principles to the best of their abilities recognising that to honour and observe them makes for a more peaceful world, with greater loving-kindness.

Needless to say, we often fail dismally in living up to these standards, which is why we find ourselves in lives fraught with corruption, depravity, selfishness and arrogance. However, even those who are most painfully conscious of how short they fall from leading a fully virtuous life would never suggest, for that reason alone, that the principles to which they keep so imperfectly should be disregarded.

Obviously, to regret our capacity to do good as we would wish

4. The Six Perfections, or *paramitas*, may not perhaps be as familiar to some readers. They comprise: *dana* (generosity, giving of oneself); *shila* (virtue, morality, discipline, proper conduct); *kshanti* (patience, tolerance, forbearance, acceptance, endurance); *virya* (energy, diligence, vigour, effort); *dhyana* (contemplation, concentration) and; *prajna* (wisdom, insight).

does not mean that we are incapable of any good at all or what others may consider to be 'good'. This qualification is necessary because acts that are praised as morally admirable by others are not always considered so by the doer. However, behaviour that is sometimes judged as thoroughly laudable by observers could, in fact, be motivated by the deepest self-interest in the person being praised. They may, for instance, want to be highly regarded or admired by their peers, to allay perhaps a sense of guilt over something, or to avoid censure or humiliation in not doing what is expected of a 'good person' in particular circumstances.

However, we are also aware of instinctive and guileless acts of kindness that do not seem contrived or cynical. These are usually the exception as they often go completely against one's own advantage. Such behaviour, then, appears to stem from a deeper source than our self-centred needs or the demands of social convention. At such times, when our 'small' self is temporarily suspended or kept in abeyance, we are apt to observe natural and unfeigned instances of compassion: compassion that has its wellspring in the Buddha-nature itself which lies deeply buried in all of us and which—as we have seen—discloses itself through our experience of shinjin. This gives us an important clue about the nature of morality and its relationship to religion.

Moral value is not ascribed to acts in mere virtue of their sanction by religious authority. We prize certain behaviour because, intuitively, we recognise the spark of something greater than the individual and their self-interest at work; something bright and universal.

Experience appears to confirm that real acts of moral purity, as rare as they are surprising, are never acknowledged as such by those who perform them. Such people are either oblivious to their own virtue or, perhaps, they see their own inadequacy so clearly that they are convinced that no good could possibly be found within them—which, in a sense, may well be correct since the true good that others see has its source elsewhere.

This points to compassion as the essence of moral virtue and true compassion cannot be experienced except through that which makes it possible in the first place—the wisdom in which is revealed our deep connection to all beings as manifestations of one infinite reality.

> For all sentient beings, without exception, have been our parents, brothers and sisters in the course of countless lives in the many states of existence.
>
> —*A Record in Lament of Divergences*

Morality must, ultimately, have its foundation in spiritual realisation; otherwise, it will fluctuate according to taste or custom, having no real binding force on our lives or those of others.

Genuine ethical actions, therefore, are ends in themselves. We do not observe moral principles in order to advance our interests or be rewarded—this would be perverse. Our moral life must be, to the extent possible, free, uncalculated and almost unconscious, even while it is informed and sustained by our awareness of Amida Buddha's compassion towards us.

Human behaviour is, of course, inherently complex and ambiguous, and to lead a spiritual life does not, perforce, entail having clarity on all ethical problems, if for no other reason than the facts will not always be clear to us. Therefore, we need to distinguish cases of truly uncontrived kindness from those where doing the right thing depends on knowing the actual circumstances confronting us, over and above any guidance we may seek from our 'inner light'.

From the Buddhist perspective, however, the paramount consideration must be *ahimsa*, the principle of refraining from causing pain or harm to any living creature. And, yet, we frequently fail to observe this all-important injunction through the suffering that we often bring upon others, including loved ones—not necessarily out of malice but simply from abysmal ignorance or emotional confusion. Our muddled human nature rarely affords us a clear path in this sphere of life (or, indeed, in any matters of the heart).

To return to the question of morality and religion, it should be apparent that specific examples of what is perceived as ethical conduct afford no evidence, whatsoever, of any spiritual impetus behind them. We often wear masks to conceal our darker motives and we should never assume that someone whose actions appear beyond reproach is a person with an exalted moral outlook. They could just as easily be hypocrites or harbouring abhorrent desires that have yet to surface through their acts.

Even the quintessential example often given of supreme self-sacrifice—that which arises from maternal love—is not always what it seems. A mother's innate drive to protect her child is not normally extended to other children; after all, the child is a natural extension of her own being and life and, therefore, an expression of her attachment (in terms of what the child means to the mother's identity). A truly compassionate perspective—of which ordinary people are simply incapable—would consider all living beings with the same concern.

> The Buddha's regard for each sentient being with eyes of compassion is equal, as though each one was the Buddha's only child. —Genshin

The experience of shinjin can have vital implications for our way of life. With the awareness of the true nature of our unenlightened self in the light of Amida Buddha's wisdom, the worst excesses of our ego can be seen clearly and, in many cases, attenuated. Our self-attachment is still there but the recognition of its toxic nature leads us to gain a measure of sobriety in relation to it as well as develop some distance from its pitfalls, thereby helping us alleviate the 'sting in the tail' of our blind passions. In doing so, we have a heightened sense of our moral failings—regardless of what others may think of us—because we have become sensitised to the purity of the Buddha's light, in contrast to which our grievous shortcomings become all the more apparent.

This is not cause for any kind of guilt or self-contempt. Rather, our natural response is one of regret, remorse and serious reflection on the impact of our often thoughtless and hurtful actions. We say 'regret' rather than 'guilt' because of our inescapable imperfections and the inherent fragility of human beings. People without this perspective may be oblivious to their detrimental impact in the world, convinced of their own decency and rectitude in all things.

In view of this, Shin Buddhism, with its starkly honest and uncompromising assessment of human nature, declares that moral faultlessness—if indeed it has ever existed among mere mortals—is in no way a prerequisite for leading a spiritual life. To try to perfect that which is inherently flawed is futile and to insist on doing so can only cause grave harm.

Having said that, we must admit the possibility that authentically benevolent behaviour may emerge in a person, notwithstanding the general moral bewilderment and perplexity to which we are all subject. This is comparable to the true nembutsu that is exclaimed from the depths of our being – something for which we cannot take any credit and which rightly belongs to the Buddha alone.

Conclusions along these lines have led critics to suppose that Shin remains lax with respect to personal conduct, in view of its belief that—as shinjin is sufficient for our spiritual emancipation—immorality is not an obstacle to attaining Nirvana. Perhaps the final word on this matter should rest with Shinran:

> Maddened beyond control by blind passions, we do things we should not, say things we should not and think things we should not. But if a person is deceitful in his relations with others, doing what he should not and saying what he should not because he thinks it will not hinder his birth (in the Pure Land), then it is not an instance of being maddened by passion. Since he purposely does these things, they are simply misdeeds that should never have been done.
>
> Formerly you were drunk with the wine of ignorance and had a liking only for the three poisons of greed, anger and folly but, since you have begun to hear of the Buddha's Vow, you have gradually awakened from the drunkenness of ignorance, gradually rejected the three poisons and have come to prefer, at all times, the medicine of Amida Buddha.
>
> It is indeed sorrowful to give way to impulses with the excuse that one is by nature possessed of blind passions—excusing acts that should not be committed, words that should not be said and thoughts that should not be harboured—and to say that one may follow one's desires in any way whatsoever. It is like offering more wine before a person has become sober or urging him to take even more poison before it has abated. 'Here's some medicine, so drink all the poison you like'—words like these should never be said.
>
> In people who have long heard the Buddha's Name and said the nembutsu, surely there are signs of rejecting the evil of this world and signs of their desire to cast off the evil in themselves.

Let us move on to the matter of our emotional life. While many people are apt to play down their emotions or not give them their full due, it is clear that insufficient attention to this aspect of our lives can have a noxious effect on our well-being. Not only that, but an emotional life uninformed by some measure of spiritual realisation can only compound the problems that suppressed or untamed emotions can cause in our lives.

Though not, perhaps, immediately obvious, the awakening of shinjin can vivify the emotional dimension of our existence. Encountering the reality of Amida Buddha makes us see the true source of all those things that we treasure in our relationships with others such as love, tenderness, affection and trust. Ordinarily, while such feelings can go awry and cause distress through abuse or frailty, they also point to a deep need that we have for warmth, acceptance and understanding. Such needs, of course, are often unmet in our lives.

We sometimes feel that our happiness relies on being with a particular person or having certain kinds of friends. When we fail to have such people in our lives, or when they abandon us, we can be overwhelmed by resentment or grief. We try, as best as we can, to mend our broken hearts but we may be driven to forsake the quest for emotional fulfilment altogether.

Our emotions are notoriously complicated and perplexing, and often subject to contradictions that cannot easily be resolved. They are messy, yet an integral part of what makes us human. We seek to satisfy our emotional needs in so many ways but we often find ourselves groping in the dark. We sometimes feel that we have lost our bearings or that we need some kind of compass to help us find our true destination in life. Failure to do so can lead to anxiety and pain. It is a sad and deeply poignant fact that many go to the grave with crippled or unfulfilled emotional lives: battered, confused and disappointed.

To be sure, we are quite capable of experiencing moments of emotional exultation but these, unfortunately, are not always stable or enduring. The very occasion that gave us such pleasure or excitement a week ago may repel us today. Unless grounded in something deeper, our emotions can become extremely fickle and uncertain; they can also easily be inflamed by anger, fear, envy and jealousy.

The fundamental difficulty of being human is often reflected in the unruly and tumultuous world of our emotional life. Can so powerful a need for what emotional fulfilment promises be based on just a vagary of human temperament and conditioning? Are these impulses simply blind and inexplicable, destined never to be satisfied? What really lies behind our thirst for emotional prosperity?

These questions take us back to our discussion in the first chapter, where we spoke about the significance of yearning in relation to spiritual reality. Could our connection to this reality also have a bearing on our emotional health?

> The light of the Buddha of Unhindered Light
> Harbours the lights of purity, joy and wisdom;
> Its virtuous working surpasses conceptual understanding,
> As it benefits beings throughout the ten quarters.
>
> —Shinran

Shinran's note to this hymn reads as follows:

> —*Unhindered*: not obstructed by karmic evil and blind passions.
>
> —*Purity, joy and wisdom*: since it saves one from greed, it is called 'purity'. Since it saves one from anger, it is called 'joy'. Since it saves one from folly, it is called 'wisdom'.

Who can deny that a great deal of our emotional energy is steeped in greed, anger and folly? As much as we try to seek meaningful and rewarding interactions with people, we find that they can be mired in 'blind passions'. And yet we continue undeterred, striving—in our nobler moments—for 'purity, joy and wisdom' in our relationships with others.

In seeking emotional rewards, we continue to focus on what we can get for ourselves, aiming to serve our most pressing needs and interests. Of course, it is natural to do so but we need to be mindful of the disagreeable limitations in living this way.

As the real essence of all those values that we seek in our emotional quest, Amida Buddha is able to provide us with a firm and lasting foundation of inner weal throughout our lives: something that we seek in so many other ways but which is often realised imperfectly and in a way that comes mixed with sorrow.

This does not mean that we repudiate our earthly joys because of their tendency to fall short of our expectations. On the contrary, only by experiencing the full range of which human love is capable are we able, perhaps, to awaken to a deeper love that underlies all others and unifies them; lending to our ordinary affections a richer dimension, which enlivens them and makes them shine with a radiance that goes beyond our frequently self-absorbed and narrow infatuations.

Amida Buddha's pure light can refine our ordinary emotions and the turmoil that fuels them by allowing us to see that the deepest longings of our heart can be completely fulfilled by this undying reality through which all hopes and desires are perfectly consummated, and all conflicts resolved. This is not unworldly escapism. It is the illumination, by the Buddha's wisdom, of the mass of confusion that makes up our commonplace lives.

> Even when we are evil, if we revere the power of the Vow all the more deeply, gentle-heartedness and forbearance will surely arise in us through its spontaneous working.
>
> —*A Record in Lament of Divergences*

In a practical sense, this means that we should seek and nurture the traces of the Buddha's light in the world wherever we can find them, in all the devotions and hankerings that animate and give purpose to our lives, but in a way that recognises their constraints and propensity to go astray.

The light of Amida pervades our lives even when we are in the throes of the most dire passions. As precious as they are to us, our human joys and loves—while partaking something of the blissfulness of Nirvana (for they have no other origin)—cannot fully meet our deepest human need to be unconditionally embraced and accepted, which is precisely what Amida vows to do for all beings.

> Sentient beings who solely think on Amida Buddha . . . are constantly illumined by the light of that Buddha's heart, grasped and protected, never to be abandoned. . . .
>
> —Shan-tao

In this way, we are able to derive profound consolation from the fact that in moments of either exhilaration or sadness, the Buddha's beneficent presence is available to us at all times. When our desires are frustrated or thwarted, we can take refuge in the Infinite Light that nurtured them in the first place; that lit them from within and which also carries us beyond them. Even when all the things the world can give are irretrievably wrenched from us, we will always have this light shining in our hearts. This can never be taken away.

Our final topic touches on another dimension of 'applied' Buddhism that is often neglected in a spiritual climate dominated by an exclusive concern with ethics and meditation. While it may seem a little old-fashioned, a consideration of the role of beauty in our life is essential in ensuring a truly rewarding existence.

> It is told that once Ananda, the beloved disciple of Buddha, saluted his master and said: 'Half the holy life, O master, is friendship with the beautiful, association with the beautiful,

> communion with the beautiful'. 'Say not so, Ananda, say not so!' the master replied. 'It is not half of the holy life. It is the whole of the holy life.' —*Samyutta Nikaya*

Among the stern realities of our competitive, stressful and demanding world, we need to make room for the aesthetic which can inject freshness, light and harmony into our hardened lives.

In speaking this way, we are clearly not referring to matters of taste but to something that is, ultimately, imperishable and liberating. Beauty gives us respite from our hidebound views, from the mediocrity of our vapid obsessions, and from the cluttered chaos of our over-active brains and anarchic impulses. It also provides a precious haven from the barrage of noise and ugliness that so disfigures modern life.

The presence of beauty is the reality of the supreme Dharma-Body erupting forth into our world of forms; it is the blissfulness of Nirvana reaching out and whispering something of its essence to us.

> The intrinsic nature of beauty must be related to that which is eternal . . . to the world of the sacred. . . . Faith and beauty are but different aspects of the Absolute Reality . . . a manifestation of the ultimate. . . . True beauty is the form of 'Suchness'. —Yanagi

This is shown by the fact that our most powerful impressions of beauty impart a sense of serene felicity that can transform and renew our lives. We become opened up to a higher realm of being—something felt as divine—in the very midst of this world.

As we have already seen, the depictions of the Pure Land in the sutras are replete with aesthetic references. In order to convey a hint of the beatitude of Nirvana, the reader is presented with a magnificent array of images, colours, fragrances, tactile delights and sounds. Indeed, Shinran gives Amida Buddha the name 'Music of Purity' in the following hymn on the Pure Land:

> The delicate, wondrous sounds of jewel-trees in the
> jewel-forests
> Produce natural music, serene and consonant;
> Unexcelled in subtlety, pathos, grace and elegance.
> So take refuge in the Music of Purity.

We must not forget that, while Amida Buddha is unveiled in our hearts through the experience of shinjin, this is not the only means by which the Infinite discloses itself. As it pervades all reality, Amida's light seeks to reach us in every conceivable way, even through the most seemingly humble or uneventful experiences: the enchanting smile of an infant, a moving adagio by Bach, the regal gait of a lion, a breathtaking sunset over snow-covered mountains, the haunting sound of trees caressed by the wind, the awe induced by a tempestuous ocean, a melancholy bird call, or the longing glance of one's beloved.

Such encounters—which we have all had in some measure—prompt us to enter the world of the aesthetic in the true meaning of the word, namely that which appeals not just to our physical senses but to our feelings; what we perceive in our hearts and how we react emotionally. These broad-ranging experiences are invariably described as 'beautiful'—but what does this really mean?

Many thinkers simply dismiss this notion as having no objective reality, a phenomenon that is completely personal and which reflects mere individual fancy. However, anybody who has had an overpowering encounter with beauty strongly believes otherwise.

What we feel, in fact, is that we have been privileged with an experience that is greater than us and which connects us to something sublime, mysterious and ineffable: a sense of rapture that no biological reductionism can trivialise or belittle. In these experiences lies proof that, amidst the uncertainties and perplexities of the world, we can be enveloped in the calm and blessedness that beauty is able to bestow on us: a grace that we do not expect or feel we deserve. This is yet another way of living in the presence of Amida Buddha here and now.

The impact of our strongest aesthetic experiences impresses on us that this is not just another delusion or fabrication of the mind. The compelling nature of beauty cannot but inspire in us the sense that it is permeated by the highest reality—Infinite Light and Life. The intensity, passion and love that we feel in the face of beauty are, as Plato rightly discerned, a reflection in our hearts of the longing we have for union with this reality.

This suggests that the aesthetic and the spiritual are intimately related; indeed, each reflects and nourishes the other. By honouring the beauty in the world, we are able to integrate—in the most direct way—the life of Amida Buddha into our own. Beauty connects us, much more so than morality, to the very heart of things and is not the spiritual contemplation of beauty a powerful meditation in itself?

EPILOGUE

Whenever I see cherry blossoms
Bloom in profusion,
My yearning increases
For the Other Shore.

—*Rennyo*

Epilogue

It is time we discarded the tired view of Buddhism as a dry and forensic rationalism, lacking in warmth and devotion; the flawed belief that its aim is simply to promote the 'development' of the individual through practices designed to strip us of everything that makes us real people. This is a travesty of its teachings and fails to do justice to the rich and baffling complexity of human experience.

The Buddhist path seeks to immerse us in a tremendous mystery marked by an abiding peace and stillness; a quietude that is not of this world. It also leads us to discover our true identity which demands that we relinquish all that we are to the realm of the spirit, which is beyond our immediate grasp, beyond our small-minded schemes for personal gain, and beyond the self-deception that enslaves itself to empty dreams.

We must not fear plunging into the unknown: treasures are to be found at the bottom of the ocean, not scattered on its surface. The real conquest of the self cannot be sought in its incessant cultivation but in its joyful abandonment, through the unerring knowledge of that which is timeless and which beguiles us, ineluctably, to transcend ourselves.

By hearing the call of Amida Buddha we become awakened to true reality and its unfathomable working. We are urged to lift our heavy gaze from the endlessly troublesome cares that consume us in this world and to live a life that dances jubilantly in the resplendent light of the Infinite.

It is hard for us to abandon this old home of pain, where we have been transmigrating for innumerable aeons down to the present, and we feel no longing for the Pure Land of peace where we have yet to be born. Truly, how powerful our blind passions are! But though we feel reluctant to part from this world, at the moment our karmic bonds to it are exhausted and helplessly we die, we shall go to that land. Amida pities especially the person who has no thought of wanting to go there quickly. Reflecting on this, we feel the Vow of Great Compassion to be all the more trustworthy and realise that our birth in the Pure Land is settled.

—*Shinran*

References

The quotations in this book are drawn from the following sources and have, where appropriate, been slightly adapted for ease of readability. They have also been rendered into British English consistent with the style observed in the rest of this work.

CHAPTER ONE

Page 2: Venerable Master Hsuan Hua, *The Vajra Prajna Paramita Sutra: A General Explanation* (Burlingame: Buddhist Text Translation Society, 2002), p.74.

Pages 3–4: Hisao Inagaki, *The Three Pure Land Sutras* [hereafter *TPLS*] (Kyoto: Nagata Bunshodo, 2000), pp.282–286 (*passim*) and p.304.

Page 16: *TPLS*, p. 288.

CHAPTER TWO

Page 21: Bhikkhu Bodhi, trans. *The Connected Discourses of the Buddha: A New Translation of the Samyutta Nikaya* (Boston: Wisdom Publications, 2000), pp. 1378–1379.

Page 22: *The Collected Works of Shinran* [hereafter *CWS*] (Kyoto: Jodo Shinsu Hongwanji-ha, 1997), vol. 1, p. 188.

Page 23: *CWS*, vol. 1, p.164.

Page 24: D.T. Suzuki, *Outlines of Mahayana Buddhism* (New York: Schocken, 1963), pp. 223–224.

Page 25: Quoted in Helmuth von Glasenapp's *Buddhism: A Non-Theistic Religion* (New York: George Braziller, 1966), p. 83; *The Awakening of Faith: Attributed to Asvaghosha*, translated, with commentary, by Yoshito S. Hakeda (New York: Columbia University Press, 1967), p. 32; *CWS*, vol. 1, p. 461.

Page 26: *TPLS*, p. 263; *CWS*, vol. 1, p. 201; D.T. Suzuki, *The Essence of Buddhism* (London: The Buddhist Society, 1957), p. 46.

Page 27: *TPLS*, p. 236; ibid., p. 236; ibid., p. 237; ibid., pp. 238–239; ibid., p. 251.

Pages 27–28: *TPLS*, pp. 251–252.

Pages 28–29: *TPLS*, pp. 253–254.

Page 29: *CWS*, vol. 1, p. 191.

Page 31: *TPLS*, p. 251.

Page 32: *CWS*, vol. 1, pp. 460–461.

Page 33: *CWS*, vol. 1, p. 510; ibid., p. 191.

Pages 33–34: *TPLS*, p. 255.

Page 34: *CWS*, vol. 1, p. 325; ibid., p. 327.

CHAPTER THREE

Pages 40–41: *CWS*, vol. 1, p. 94.

Page 42: *CWS*, vol. 1, p. 69; ibid., p. 84.

Page 44: *CWS*, vol. 1, p. 84.

Pages 44–45: *CWS*, vol. 2, p. 172.

References

Page 45: *CWS*, vol. 2, p. 184.

Pages 45–46: *TPLS*, p. 243.

Page 46: *CWS*, vol. 1, p. 525.

Page 47: *CWS*, vol. 1, pp. 674–675; ibid., p. 459.

Page 48: *CWS*, vol. 1, p. 185; ibid., p. 351.

Page 49: *CWS*, vol. 1, p. 463; ibid., p. 299; ibid., p. 192.

Page 50: *CWS*, vol. 1, p. 326; ibid., p. 341, p. 153.

Page 51: *TPLS*, p. 263; *CWS*, vol. 1, p. 107.

Page 52: *CWS*, vol. 1, p. 497.

Page 53: *CWS*, vol. 1, p. 553; *Shozomatsu Wasan: Hymns on the Last Age* (Kyoto: Ryukoku University Press, 1980), p. 36.

Page 54: *CWS*, vol. 1, p. 661.

Page 55: Hakeda, p. 34.

Page 56: *Shozomatsu Wasan: Hymns on the Last Age* (Kyoto: Ryukoku University Press, 1980), p. 37.

Page 57: *CWS*, vol. 1, p. 13; ibid., p. 48.

Page 58: *Rennyo Shonin Kenkyu* ['A Selection from the Poems of Rennyo Shonin'] ed. by Jodoshinshu Kyogaku Kenkyusho (Kyoto: Nagata Bunshodo, 1998). Poem No. 10 translated by Hisao Inagaki.

Page 59: *CWS*, vol. 1, p. 452.

Page 60: *CWS*, vol. 1, p. 693.

CHAPTER FOUR

Page 67: *CWS*, vol. 1, p. 664.

Page 68: *CWS*, vol. 1, p. 52.

Page 70: *CWS*, vol. 1, p. 547, p. 553 (*passim*).

Page 72: *CWS*, vol. 1, p. 340; ibid., p. 341.

Page 73: *CWS*, vol. 1, p. 676.

Page 74: *CWS*, vol. 1, p. 478.

Pages 74–75: From the *Samyuta Nikaya*, quoted in the Introduction to *The Dhammapada: The Path of Perfection*, translated by Juan Mascaro (Harmondsworth: Penguin Books, 1983), pp. 20–21.

Page 75: Soetsu Yanagi, "The Dharma Gate of Beauty" (tr. Bernard Leach) in *The Eastern Buddhist* 12/2 (1979), pp. 4, 9; *The Unknown Craftsman: A Japanese Insight into Beauty* (Tokyo & New York: Kodansha International, 1989), p. 215.

Page 76: *CWS*, vol. 1, p. 334.

Further Reading

Primary Sources

EARLY BUDDHISM

The Dhammapada, tr. Gil Fronsdal (Boston: Shambala, 2006).

The Long Discourses of the Buddha: A Translation of the Digha Nikaya, tr. Maurice Walshe (Somerville: Wisdom Publications, 1995).

The Middle Length Discourses of the Buddha: A Translation of the Majjhima Nikaya, tr. Bhikkhu Nanamoli (Somerville: Wisdom Publications, 1995).

The Connected Discourses of the Buddha: A Translation of the Samyutta Nikaya, tr. Bikkhu Bodhi (Somerville: Wisdom Publications, 2002).

Abhidharma Kosa Bhasyam tr. Louis de la Vallee Poussin & Leo M. Pruden (4 vols. Fremont: Asian Humanities Press, 1990).

MAHAYANA BUDDHISM

The Awakening of Faith in the Mahayana, tr. Yoshito S. Hakeda (New York: Columbia University Press, 2005).

The Mahayana Mahaparinirvana Sutra, tr. Kosho Yamamoto, ed. & rev. Tony Page (Quebec: F. Lepine Publishing, 2008).

The Tathagatagarbha Sutra, tr. William H. Grosnick in *Buddhism in Practice* ed. Donald S. Lopez (Princeton: Princeton University Press, 1995).

The Lion's Roar of Queen Srimala: A Buddhist scripture on the Tathagatagarbha theory, tr. Alex Wayman (New York: Columbia University Press, 1974).

A Study on the Ratnagotravibhaga (*Uttaratantra*): *Being a treatise on the Tathagatagarbha theory of Mahayana Buddhism*, tr. Jikido Takasaki (Rome: Istituto Italiano per il Medio ed Estremo Oriente, 1966).

The Flower Ornament Scripture: A Translation of the Avatamsaka Sutra, tr. Thomas Cleary (Boston: Shambala, 1993).

The Lankavatara Sutra: A Mahayana Text, tr. Daisetz T. Suzuki (New Delhi: Motilal Banarsidass, 1999).

Summary of the Great Vehicle, tr. John P. Keenan (Berkeley: Numata Center for Buddhist Translation & Research, 1993).

The Lotus Sutra, tr. Burton Watson (New York: Columbia University Press, 1993).

The Large Sutra on Perfect Wisdom, tr. Edward Conze (Berkeley: University of California Press, 1975).

Perfect Wisdom: The Short Prajnaparamita Texts, tr. Edward Conze (London: Luzac, 1973).

The Sovereign All-Creating Mind, tr. by E.K. Neumaier-Dargyay (Albany: State University of New York Press, 1992).

Inquiry into the Origin of Humanity: An Annotated Translation of Tsung-Mi's Yüan jen lun with a Modern Commentary, tr. Peter N. Gregory (Honolulu: University of Hawaii Press, 1995).

PURE LAND BUDDHISM

The Three Pure Land Sutras, tr. Hisao Inagaki (Kyoto: Nagata Bunshodo, 2000).

Further Reading

The Three Pure Land Sutras, vol. I: *The Sutra on Amida Buddha and The Sutra of Contemplation on the Buddha of Immeasurable Life*, tr. Hisao Inagaki, Michio Tokunaga, Nobuo Nomura and Gene H. Sekiya (Kyoto: Jodo Shinshu Hongwanji-ha, 2003).

The Three Pure Land Sutras, vol. II: *The Sutra on the Buddha of Immeasurable Life*, tr. Hisao Inagaki, Michio Tokunaga, Nobuo Nomura, Wayne S. Yokoyama, Hidenori Kiyomoto and Gene H. Sekiya (Kyoto: Jodo Shinshu Hongwanji-ha, 2009).

Sutra of Contemplation on the Buddha of Immeasurable Life, tr. Ryukoku Translation Center (Kyoto: Ryukoku University, 1984).

Nagarjuna's Discourse on the Ten Stages tr. Hisao Inagaki (Kyoto: Nagata Bunshodo, 1998).

T'an-luan's Commentary on Vasubandhu's Discourse on the Pure Land, tr. Hisao Inagaki (Kyoto: Nagata Bunshodo, 1998).

Shan-tao's Method of Contemplation on Amida, tr. Hisao Inagaki (Kyoto: Nagata Bunshodo, 2005).

Honen's Collection of Passages on the Nembutsu Chosen in the Original Vow, tr. Morris J. Augustine and Tessho Kondo (Berkeley: Numata Center for Buddhist Translation and Research, 1997).

Plain Words on the Pure Land Way: Sayings of the Wandering Monks of Medieval Japan, tr. Dennis Hirota (Kyoto: Ryukoku University 1989).

No Abode: The Record of Ippen, tr. Dennis Hirota (Honolulu: University of Hawaii Press, 1998).

SHIN BUDDHISM

The Collected Works of Shinran, tr. Dennis Hirota, Hisao Inagaki, Michio Tokunaga and Ryushin Uryuzu (2 vols. Kyoto: Jodo Shinsu Hongwanji-ha, 1997).

Jodo Wasan 'Hymns on the Pure Land', tr. Ryukoku Translation Center (Kyoto: Ryukoku University, 1965).

Kyo Gyo Shin Sho 'Teaching, Practice, Faith and Enlightenment', tr. Ryukoku Translation Center (Kyoto: Ryukoku University, 1966).

Shoshin Ge 'Gatha of True Faith in the Nembutsu', tr. Ryukoku Translation Center (Kyoto: Ryukoku University, 1966).

Koso Wasan 'Hymns on the Patriarchs', tr. Ryukoku Translation Center (Kyoto: Ryukoku University, 1974).

Shozomatsu Wasan 'Hymns on the Last Age', tr. Ryukoku Translation Center (Kyoto: Ryukoku University, 1980).

Tanni Sho 'Notes Lamenting Differences', tr. Ryukoku Translation Center (Kyoto: Ryukoku University, 1980).

Gobunsho 'Letters of Rennyo', tr. Gadjin M. Nagao et al. (Kyoto: Hongwanji International Center, 2000).

Goichidaiki-kikigaki 'Thus I Have Heard From Rennyo Shonin', tr. Hisao Inagaki (Craiova: Dharma Lion Publications, 2008).

OTHER

Plato, *The Symposium* tr. Robin Waterfield (Oxford: Oxford University Press, 1998).

Secondary Sources

GENERAL BUDDHISM

Conze, Edward, *Buddhism: Its Essence and Development* (New York: Harper & Row, 1975).

Coomaraswamy, Ananda K., *Buddha and the Gospel of Buddhism* (New Delhi: Munshiram Manoharlal, 1985).

Harvey, Peter, *An Introduction to Buddhism: Teachings, History and Practices* (Cambridge: Cambridge University Press, 1990).

Schumann, Hans Wolfgang, *Buddhism: An Outline of its Teachings and Schools,* tr. Georg Feuerstein (Wheaton: Quest Books, 1987).

Takasaki, Jikido, *An Introduction to Buddhism,* tr. Rolf W. Giebel (Tokyo: Toho Gakkai, 1987).

von Glasenapp, Helmuth, *Buddhism: A Non-Theistic Religion,* tr. Irmgard Schloegl (New York: George Braziller, 1966).

MAHAYANA BUDDHISM

Brown, Brian E., *The Buddha Nature: A Study of the Tathagatagarbha and Alayavijnana* (Delhi: Motilal Banarsidass, 1991).

McGovern, William Montgomery, *An Introduction to Mahayana Buddhism* (New Delhi: Munshiram Manoharlal, 1997).

Pallis, Marco, *A Buddhist Spectrum* (London: George Allen & Unwin, 1980).

Schuon, Frithjof, *Treasures of Buddhism* (Bloomington: World Wisdom, 1993).

Sebastien, C.D., *Metaphysics and Mysticism in Mahayana Buddhism* (Delhi: Sri Satguru Publications, 2005).

Suzuki, Beatrice Lane, *Mahayana Buddhism* (London: George Allen & Unwin, 1981).

Suzuki, Daisetz T., *Outlines of Mahayana Buddhism* (New Delhi: Munshirm Manoharlal, 2000).

Takakusu, Junjiro, *The Essentials Of Buddhist Philosophy*, ed. Wing-tsit Chan and Charles A. Moore (New Delhi: Motilal Banarsidass, 2002).

Williams, Paul, *Mahayana Buddhism: The Doctrinal Foundations* (London: Routledge, 2008).

Yamaguchi, Susumu, *Mahayana Way to Buddhahood: Theology of Enlightenment* (Los Angeles & Tokyo: Buddhist Books International, 1982).

PURE LAND BUDDHISM

Andrews, Allan, *The Teachings Essential for Rebirth: A Study of Genshin's Ojoyoshu* (Tokyo: Sophia University, 1973).

Fitzgerald, Joseph (ed.), *Honen the Buddhist Saint* (Bloomington: World Wisdom, 2006).

Fujiwara, Ryosetsu, *The Way to Nirvana: The Concept of the Nembutsu in Shan-tao's Pure Land Buddhism* (Tokyo: The Kyoiku Shincho Sha, 1974).

Ingram, Paul O., *The Dharma of Faith: An Introduction to Classical Pure Land Buddhism* (Washington: University Press of America, 1977).

Further Reading

SHIN BUDDHISM

Andreasen, Esben, *Popular Buddhism in Japan: Shin Buddhist Religion & Culture* (Honolulu: University of Hawaii Press, 1997).

Arai, Toshikazu, *Grasped by the Buddha's Vow* (San Francisco: Buddhist Churches of America, 2008).

Bloom, Alfred, *Shinran's Gospel of Pure Grace* (Tuscon: University of Arizona, 1965).

Bloom, Alfred, *Tannisho: A Resource for Modern Living* (Honolulu: Buddhist Study Center Press, 1981).

Bloom, Alfred, *Shoshinge: The Heart of Shin Buddhism* (Honolulu: Honpa Hongwanji Mission of Hawaii, 1986).

Bloom, Alfred, *The Life of Shinran Shonin: The Journey to Self-Acceptance* (Berkeley: Institute of Buddhist Studies, 1994).

Bloom, Alfred, *The Promise of Boundless Compassion: Shin Buddhism for Today* (Honolulu: Buddhist Study Center Press, 2003).

Bloom, Alfred, *The Essential Shinran: A Buddhist Path of True Entrusting* (Bloomington: World Wisdom, 2007).

Dobbins, James C., *Jodo Shinshu: Shin Buddhism in Medieval Japan* (Honolulu: University of Hawaii Press, 2002).

Fujii, Ryuchi, *The True Meaning of Buddhism* (Kyoto: Honpa Hongwanji Press, 1957).

Fujimoto, Ryukyo, *An Outline of the Triple Sutra of Shin Buddhism* (Kyoto: Honpa Hongwanji Press, vol. 1, 1955, vol. 2, 1960).

Gatenby, George & Paraskevopoulos, John, *A Primer of Shin Buddhism* (Sydney: Hongwanji Buddhist Mission of Australia, 1995).

Hanada, Russell & Kodani, Masao, *Traditions of Jodoshinshu Hongwanji-ha* (Los Angeles: Senshin Buddhist Temple, 1984).

Hirota, Dennis & Ueda, Yoshifumi, *Shinran: An Introduction to His Thought* (Kyoto: Hongwanji International Center, 1989).

Hirota, Dennis, *Asura's Harp: Engagement with Language as a Buddhist Path* (Heidelberg: Universitätsverlag, 2006).

Inaba, Shuken & Funabashi, Issai, *Jodo Shinshu: An Introduction to the Authentic Pure Land Teaching*, tr. Ichirai Fukuhara & William Flygare (Kyoto: Otani University 1961).

Inagaki, Hisao (ed.), *A Glossary of Shin Buddhist Terms* (Kyoto: Nagata Bunshodo, 1995).

Inagaki, Hisao, *Amida the Infinite: An Introduction to Shin Buddhism* (Adelaide: Horai Association of Australia, 2000).

Inagaki, Hisao, *The Way of Nembutsu-Faith* (Kyoto: Nagata Bunshodo, 2000).

Inagaki, Zuiken S., *Anjin* (Kyoto: Nagata Bunshodo, 1988).

Itsuki, Hiroyuki, *Tariki: Embracing Despair, Discovering Peace* (New York: Kodansha America, 2001).

Kakehashi, Jitsuen, *Bearer of the Light: The Life and Thought of Rennyo* (Los Angeles: Pure Land Publications, 1999).

Kanamatsu, Kenryo, *Naturalness: A Classic of Shin Buddhism* (Bloomington: World Wisdom, 2002).

Kobai, Eiken, *Understanding Jodo-Shinhsu* (Los Angeles: Nembutsu Press, 1998).

Kobai, Eiken, *Misunderstandings of Master Rennyo* (Los Angeles: Nembutsu Press, 1998).

Kobai, Eiken, *True and Real World of Salvation: An Introduction to the Life and Teaching of the Venerable Master Shinran* (Craiova: Dharma Lion Publications, 2007).

Lloyd, Arthur, *Shinran and his work: Studies in Shinshu Theology* (Tokyo: Kyobunkwan, 1910).

Matsumoto, Shoji & Tabrah, Ruth, *The Natural Way of Shin Buddhism* (Honolulu: Buddhist Study Center Press, 1993).

Nakai, Gendo, *Shinran and his Religion of Pure Faith* (Kyoto: Shinshu Research Institute, 1937).

Porcu, Elisabetta, *Pure Land Buddhism in Modern Japanese Culture* (Leiden & Boston: Brill, 2008).

Rogers, Minor & Ann, *Rennyo: The Second Founder of Shin Buddhism* (Fremont: Asian Humanities Press, 1991).

Seki, Hozen, *The Great Natural Way* (New York: American Buddhist Academy, 1976).

Shigaraki, Takamoro, *An Introduction to Shin Buddhism*, tr. Toshikazu Arai and Claire Ichiyama (Honolulu: Buddhist Study Center, 1984).

Shigaraki, Takamoro, *A Life of Awakening: The Heart of the Shin Buddhist Path*, tr. David Matsumoto (Kyoto: Hozokan Publishing, 2005).

Stewart, Harold, *By the Old Walls of Kyoto: A Year's Cycle of Landscape Poems with Prose Commentaries* (New York: Weatherhill, 1981).

Suzuki, Daisetz T., *A Miscellany of the Shin Teaching of Buddhism* (Kyoto: Shinshu Otani Shumusho, 1949).

Takahashi, Takeichi & Izumida, Junjo, *Shinranism in Mahayana Buddhism and the Modern World* (Los Angeles: Higashi Hongwanji, 1932).

Tanaka, Kenneth K., *Ocean: An Introduction to Jodo-Shinshu Buddhism in America* (Berkeley: Wisdom Ocean Publications, 1997).

Tatsuguchi, Wasui, *A Study of Shin Buddhism* (Honolulu: Shinshu Kyokai Mission of Hawaii, 1961).

Unno, Taitetsu, *River of Fire, River of Water: An Introduction to the Pure Land Tradition of Shin Buddhism* (New York: Doubleday, 1998).

Unno, Taitetsu, *Shin Buddhism: Bits of Rubble Turn into Gold* (New York: Doubleday, 2002).

Yamamoto, Kosho, *An Introduction to Shin Buddhism* (Ube: The Karinbunko, 1963).

Yamamoto, Kosho, *The Other Power* (Ube: The Karinbunko, 1965).

Yamaoka, Haruo, *The Teaching and Practice of Jodo Shinshu* (San Francisco: Buddhist Churches of America, 1974).

Author

The author is an ordained priest in the Shin tradition of Mahayana Buddhism and is engaged in a variety of both pastoral and academic activities. He holds a first-class honours degree in Philosophy from the University of Melbourne in Australia and is editor of the online *Journal of Shin Buddhism,* which has received plaudits from various international authorities as one of the most comprehensive and scholarly websites devoted to this tradition.

PUBLICATIONS

'Conceptions of the Absolute in Mahayana Buddhism and the Pure Land Way', in *Light From The East: Modern Western Encounters with Eastern Traditions* (Bloomington: World Wisdom, 2007).

'Non-Duality in Pure Land Buddhism', *Temenos Academy Review* (Issue No. 9, 2006).

'Amida's Dharma in the Modern World', *The Pure Land: Journal of the International Association of Shin Buddhist Studies* (New Series, No. 20, December 2003).

'The Nembutsu as Great Practice: Recitation of the Divine Name during the Decadent Age of the Dharma', *Sacred Web 7* (2001).

'The Awakening of Faith in the Mahayana and its Significance for Shin Buddhism', *The Pure Land: Journal of the International Association of Shin Buddhist Studies* (New Series, Nos. 13–14, December 1997).

A Primer of Shin Buddhism (with George Gatenby), (Sydney: Hongwanji Buddhist Mission of Australia, 1995).